Key Stage 3

BITESIZE
revision

Check
and test

English

Imelda Pilgrim and Brian Conroy

Published by BBC Educational Publishing,
BBC White City, 201 Wood Lane, London W12 7TS.

First published 2001   Reprinted 2002

ISBN 0 563 543566

Reproduced by Spectrum Colour, England

Printed in Italy by Poligrafico Dehoniano.

BBC

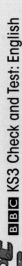

BBC KS3 Check and Test: English

Contents

www.bbc.co.uk/revision

Reading: fiction, poetry and non-fiction

About the KS3 Bitesize service

KS3 Bitesize is a revision service designed to help you achieve success in the National Tests. There are books, television programmes and a website, which can be found at **www.bbc.co.uk/revision**. It's called *Bitesize* because it breaks revision into bite-sized chunks to make it easier to learn. *Check and Test* is the latest addition to the *Bitesize* revision service.

How to use this book

This book is divided into the 100 essential things you need to know, so your revision is quick and simple. It provides a quick test for each bite-sized chunk so you can check that you know it!

Use this book to check your understanding of KS3 English.
If you can prove to yourself that you're confident with these key ideas, you'll know that you're on track with your learning.

You can use this book to test yourself:

- during your KS3 course
- at the end of the course during revision.

As you revise, you can use *Check and Test* in several ways:

- as a summary of the essential information on each of the 100 topics to help you revise those areas
- to check your revision progress: test yourself to see how confident which you are with each topic
- to keep track and plan your time: you can aim to check and test a set number of topics each time you revise, knowing how many you need to cover in total and how much time you've got.

More KS3 Bitesize resources

KS3 Bitesize Revision: English is a book that contains the key information and skills you need to revise, plus lots of tips and practice questions to help you improve your results. ISBN: 0 563 47432 7

The KS3 Bitesize Revision: English website provides even more practice and explanation to help you revise. It can be found at **www.bbc.co.uk/revision**.

Topic checker

Use the topic checkers on this page to keep track of the topics you've covered as you work through them. They're also useful to double-check that you've covered each area.

- Once you're confident with a topic and can answer the questions, you can cross the topic number off the first grid. As you check the topic for a second or third time, you can cross it off each grid.

- You'll be able to see which topics you've covered most thoroughly and those which you haven't done as much work on. Is this because you're confident that you know these topics or are you putting off looking at them?

- Any problem topics should sink in by your third check.

- Don't worry if you don't have time to go over each topic three times. Every time you look at a topic, you'll be able to remember a little bit more.

First time

1	2	3	4	5	6	7	8	9	10
11	12	13	14	15	16	17	18	19	20
21	22	23	24	25	26	27	28	29	30
31	32	33	34	35	36	37	38	39	40
41	42	43	44	45	46	47	48	49	50
51	52	53	54	55	56	57	58	59	60
61	62	63	64	65	66	67	68	69	70
71	72	73	74	75	76	77	78	79	80
81	82	83	84	85	86	87	88	89	90
91	92	93	94	95	96	97	98	99	100

Second time

1	2	3	4	5	6	7	8	9	10
11	12	13	14	15	16	17	18	19	20
21	22	23	24	25	26	27	28	29	30
31	32	33	34	35	36	37	38	39	40
41	42	43	44	45	46	47	48	49	50
51	52	53	54	55	56	57	58	59	60
61	62	63	64	65	66	67	68	69	70
71	72	73	74	75	76	77	78	79	80
81	82	83	84	85	86	87	88	89	90
91	92	93	94	95	96	97	98	99	100

Third time

1	2	3	4	5	6	7	8	9	10
11	12	13	14	15	16	17	18	19	20
21	22	23	24	25	26	27	28	29	30
31	32	33	34	35	36	37	38	39	40
41	42	43	44	45	46	47	48	49	50
51	52	53	54	55	56	57	58	59	60
61	62	63	64	65	66	67	68	69	70
71	72	73	74	75	76	77	78	79	80
81	82	83	84	85	86	87	88	89	90
91	92	93	94	95	96	97	98	99	100

BBC KS3 Check and Test: English

Check the facts

How clear is your **handwriting**? Has a teacher, parent or friend complained that they can't read it? Do you suffer from any of these handwriting concerns:

- Too large and loopy
- Letters not clearly formed
- All letters the same height
- Letters too small... or too big
- Letters pointing in different directions
- Blotchy writing?

If your writing matches any of these you need to start working on it.

Your examiner needs to be able to read your writing without having to struggle. Work out exactly what your problem is and when it's at its worst. For example, many students find that their writing is fine until they have to hurry. Others find that a new pen solves the problem.

Test yourself

Write the words of a verse of a song you know twice, once slowly and once quickly. Ask yourself:

1 Are the letters clearly formed?

2 Are the letters the right size?

3 Can all the words be read easily?

4 Does it look reasonably tidy?

Now give your writing to a parent or friend and ask them the same questions. If there's no problem, move on to unit 2. If there's something you're not happy with, **spend time practising your handwriting** at different speeds.

Focus on the area that needs improvement.

Check the facts

Most students spell most words correctly most of the time. Most students think they are poor spellers. Both of these statements are true.

How good a speller are you? Can you spot the ten deliberate mistakes in this passage? Can you correct them?

> Luke had allways wanted to be a writter. Even as a small child he would write storys to make his freinds laugh and, as he got older, he was fasinated by the storys he read. He would spend hours with his head in a book by J.K.Rowling or Phillip Pullman. His freinds thought he was crazy but Luke dident care. Throughout the long days at school his mind was bubbleing with ideas. He was determined to be a writter and that was all that mattered.

In fact there are really only seven mistakes here. The student has misspelt the same three words twice. **Most of the mistakes here could easily be avoided if the writer had applied a few basic spelling rules**:

- To spell *writer*, you take the stem word **write** and **add r**.
- To make plurals of words that end in a consonant and y you **cut off the y and add ies**, so *story* becomes *stories*.
- Knowing the rule of *i before e except after c* would have made sure that *friends* was spelt correctly.

Test yourself

1. The most common mistakes are made with words that are used often. Do you know the difference between these frequently used words that sound similar but have a different spelling and a different meaning? Use a dictionary if you're not sure.

they're	there	their
we're	where	were

Writing

BBC KS3 Check and Test: English

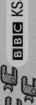

7

Check the facts

A morpheme is the smallest unit of meaning in a word.

A word may consist of one morpheme (help), two morphemes, (help/ful) or three or more morphemes (un/help/ful, un/help/ful/ly).

The main part of the word is called the stem (un**help**fully).

Prefixes are morphemes. They can be added to the beginning of a word to change its meaning.

for example:

Prefix		Stem		Word
dis	+	agree	=	disagree
pre	+	view	=	preview
un	+	kind	=	unkind

Can you identify the nineteen words with prefixes in this passage?

> The two impossible and thoroughly unhelpful girls disappeared upstairs to rethink their plans. They were unsure whether to return to the supermarket and repay what they owed or to try to exchange the goods. Feeling unhealthy, unsure and uptight they subtracted what they owed from their savings. It didn't look good. But then, by an extraordinary coincidence they discovered that their postgraduate uncle was arriving by bicycle later that day.

Prefixes have meaning, for example:
• **dis** – not or without   • **pre** – before   • **un** – not

Knowing prefixes will help you with both your spelling and your reading.

Test yourself

1 What prefixes could be attached to these words?

sincere	connect	dependent	press
edible	grade	necessary	similar
spell	take	historic	mature

2 Find out the meaning of these prefixes. Use a dictionary to help you.

extra   post   bi   re   ex   in

Check the facts

Prefixes are added to the beginning of a word. **Suffixes are added to the end of a word.** They also alter the meaning of the word, for example:

Stem		Suffix		Word
point	+	ed	=	pointed
quick	+	ly	=	quickly
walk	+	ing	=	walking

Sometimes more than one suffix can be added to a word, for example:

Stem		Suffix		Word
point	+	ed = pointed + ly	=	pointedly
hope	+	ful = hopeful + ness	=	hopefulness
deaf	+	en = deafen + ing	=	deafening

Identify the words with suffixes in this passage. Underline the stem in one colour and the suffix(es) in another. There are 17 altogether.

> The boy and girl were waiting hopefully. The older child laughed at the younger and asked him why he looked so sad. He turned his eyes to her, a look of amazement on his face. Was she being foolish? Had no-one really told her? He picked up the booklet from the floor and pointed to the picture on the front. Gazing from the cover was a portrait of their father, the kindest man they had ever known.

Knowing suffixes will help you with both your spelling and your reading.

Test yourself

1 Here are some common suffixes:

ing   ed   est   ly   ness   ation   ant   ous

How many words can you make using these suffixes and these stems?

depend   interest   courage   inform   clever

2 What suffixes could be attached to these words?

thank   brave   laugh   thought   attract

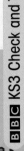

Check the facts

> **Most nouns have a singular (one)**
> **and a plural (more than one) form.**

The most common way to turn the singular into plural is to add *s*, for example:

toy – toy<u>s</u>   show – show<u>s</u>   kite – kite<u>s</u>   example – example<u>s</u>   zoo – zoo<u>s</u>

There are, however, a few other rules you need to know.

Read the passage below carefully and work out the rule for spelling the plural of words that:

- end in **ch**, e.g. chur*ch* or **sh**, e.g. bu*sh*
- end in a **vowel** and a **y**, e.g. d*ay*
- end in a **consonant** and a **y**, e.g. la*dy*

- end in **ss**, e.g. mo*ss*
- end in **x**, e.g. fo*x*
- end in **f** or **fe**, e.g. wol*f*, li*fe*

> The boys had been out on the river all through the hot summer days. Today they gazed idly beyond the bushes and mosses that lined the riverbank, to the sleepy villages with their quiet churches. The previous day they had been lucky enough to spot two foxes running across the green fields, but today the fields were empty. Two ladies they met walking reported hearing wolves the night before but they had their doubts about that. Their lives would never again be so easy and uncomplicated.

Exceptions

Some words have irregular plurals. You will already know many of these. What are the plural forms of the following words?

man   foot   child   ox   woman

Try to learn irregular plurals as you come across them.

Test yourself

1 Write the plural form of the following words:

fox	baby	thief	match
monster	life	box	loss
mouse	cow	place	tooth

2 Write the singular form of the following words:

cities	toys	ladies	stitches
misses	goals	knives	sheep

Check the facts

When you speak you don't include punctuation. At the end of a sentence you don't say 'full stop'. There's no need to. You naturally pause to make sense of what you are saying for your listener. When you ask a question you don't say 'question mark' at the end of the sentence. Instead, you raise the pitch of your voice so that it's obvious you are asking a question.

Read this passage and work out **why you need punctuation in writing**.

> have you ever considered how difficult it is to follow writing without punctuation you do not know where a sentence starts or ends and on top of that you can't work out when the writer is asking a question punctuation is there for the reader not the writer it helps the reader work through a text and understand it

Now decide where the punctuation marks should go in the passage.

Here are some of the punctuation marks that you need to know and use.

- Capital letter C
- Full stop .
- Question mark ?
- Exclamation mark !
- Comma ,

Test yourself

1 Which of the punctuation marks above indicates:
 a) surprise, anger, warning or humour
 b) a pause within a sentence
 c) the end of a complete statement
 d) the start of a sentence or a name
 e) that a question has been asked?

2 Re-write this passage using appropriate punctuation.

> have you understood this page so far if you fail to use punctuation then your words become very difficult to follow your reader becomes confused and your writing becomes less effective you must punctuate your writing if you want your reader to understand what you have written simple

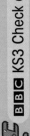

Check the facts

There are a number of other punctuation marks you need to know and use in your writing.

Read this passage. Work out the two uses for the apostrophe (').

> <u>John's</u> mother refused to listen. <u>He'd</u> told her the same story last week and, when <u>she'd</u> checked it out, it <u>hadn't</u> been true. <u>She'd</u> spoken to <u>John's</u> friend and his teachers and been shocked by what <u>she'd</u> discovered.

An apostrophe is used to show:

- that words have been shortened or contracted, for example:
  he had becomes *he'd*   *had not* becomes *hadn't*
  The apostrophe shows where the letters have been missed out.
- possession or belonging to, for example:
  the mother of John becomes *John's mother*
  the friends of John becomes *John's friends*

A colon (:) is used to:

- introduce a list, quotation, piece of speech or question, for example:
  To make this cake you need: eggs, flour, milk, chocolate and butter.
  Yesterday the manager said: 'We deeply regret what has happened.'

A semi-colon (;) is used to:

- create a pause in a sentence where a comma would be too weak and a full stop would be too strong, for example:
  The holiday was great; there were blue skies and sunshine every day.

Test yourself

1 Complete this chart with the appropriate form.

Did not	Didn't	They have	
I had			Don't
	Shouldn't	Cannot	
She will		We have	

2 Copy the semi-colon example from above. Try writing your own sentences with semi-colons, using this as a model.

Check the facts

An **ellipsis** (...) is used to:

* show that part of the text has been missed out, for example:
  William Shakespeare was born in 1564... and died in 1616.

* suggest a pause or hesitation in speech, for example:
  'I'm not sure,' she said. 'Er... would it be possible... em... could you ask for me?'

* suggest the passage of time, for example:
  Kate fell asleep without a care in the world...
  The following day when she awoke she knew instantly that things had changed.

> **Inverted commas (' ') are also known as quotation marks and speech marks.**

They are used to:

* show that a word or group of words is quoted from another text, for example:
  Lady Macbeth is determined that her husband should be king but is worried that he is 'too full o'th'milk of human kindness'.

* show words that are actually spoken, for example:
  'I'll meet you at six,' she said, anxious to get rid of him.
  'Fine. Don't be late,' he replied, already turning away.

Test yourself

1 Write a few lines of speech. Use ellipsis in it to show pauses and hesitation.

2 Re-write these sentences putting the inverted commas in the correct place.
a) One of Macbeth's most famous speeches starts with: Is this a dagger that I see before me.
b) The witches greet Macbeth as king hereafter.
c) Have you seen the play? Jackie asked excitedly.
   Sean turned and replied quietly, We're hoping to go and watch it tomorrow.

Writing

Check the facts

Sentences usually take one of three forms.

- **Simple sentences** are used to **communicate one idea**, for example:
  He went to the shops.
  They are the first kind of sentences you learn to write.

- **Compound sentences link two or more simple sentences or clauses** by using words such as **and**, **but**, and **or**. These linking words are called conjunctions. For example:
  He went to the shops *and* he bought some sweets *but* he could not get a magazine.
  Each of the clauses underlined in the example can stand as a sentence on its own.

- **Complex sentences contain a main clause** (which could stand as a sentence on its own) **and at least one subordinate clause** (which could not stand as a sentence on its own). For example:
  He went to the shops, having run out of things to do at home, but he could not get a magazine.

Test yourself

1 Identify these different sentence forms.
a) Having finally found the one she liked, she discovered they had run out of stock.
b) She could have gone to the shops but she decided not to bother.
c) They would soon be closed.
d) She would have to try again, however reluctantly, if nothing turned up within the next few days.

2 Experiment with using the conjunctions **and**, **but** and **or** to form different compound sentences by combining two or more of these simple sentences.

It was a warm day.   You could bathe in the sea.
The sun was shining.   Rain was forecast.
It would soon turn cold.   There were seashells to gather.
You could walk along the sand.   The skies were blue.

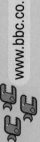

Check the facts

Read this passage.

> I went to a local school. The school was huge. There were
> over one thousand students in it. We had to wear a uniform.
> It was navy blue. I hated it. Most of the teachers were helpful.
> One or two weren't. I remember my form room clearly.
> We had register there every morning.

Whilst the writing is accurate, this student has used only **simple
sentences**. This makes it boring to read. Now read this.

> <u>With</u> over one thousand students in it, the local school
> I went to was huge. We had to wear a uniform <u>which</u> was
> navy blue. I hated it. Most of the teachers were helpful
> <u>although</u> one or two weren't. I remember my form room
> clearly <u>as</u> we had register there every morning.

Here the student has used **compound and complex sentences** to give the
same information. One short, simple sentence is kept for effect. The student
has used words to link ideas within and between sentences. These are
underlined for you. Words that work in this way can be called **connectives**.

Here is a useful list	however	finally	because
of connectives to use	so	therefore	nevertheless
in your writing:	then	after	meanwhile

Test yourself

1 Develop this passage to include:
- a range of sentence forms
- a range of connectives.

> It was a sunny day. I went to the park. The park is about
> a mile from my home. I walked there. There were many
> people in the park. Some people were lying in the
> sunshine. Others were boating on the lake. I met some
> friends there. We had a drink in the café.

2 Annotate your writing to show the different sentence forms and the
connectives you have used.

Check the facts

> A sentence usually contains a verb, which is a word that can change its tense.

In English, the present, past and future tenses can be expressed in a number of different ways. Take the verb *to walk*. A writer using the **present tense** could say:

Singular		Plural	
I walk	I am walking	we walk	we are walking
you walk	you are walking	you walk	you are walking
he (she/it) walks	he (she/it) is walking	they walk	they are walking

A writer using the **past tense** could say:

Singular		Plural	
I walked	I was walking	we walked	we were walking
you walked	you were walking	you walked	you were walking
he (she/it) walked	he (she/it) was walking	they walked	they were walking

A writer using the **future tense** could say:

Singular		Plural	
I will walk	I will be walking	we will walk	we will be walking
you will walk	you will be walking	you will walk	you will be walking
he (she/it) will walk	he (she/it) will be walking	they will walk	they will be walking

To make the past tense of a verb you usually add *d* if the word already ends in an *e*, for example, *love – loved*, and *ed* if it does not, for example *jump – jumped*. There are, however, several verbs which do not follow this pattern. For example, what is the past tense of the verb to run?

Writing

www.bbc.co.uk/revision

Test yourself

1 What present, past and future tense forms could a writer use for these verbs:

to joke

to swim

to kick

2 Copy this passage using the past tense of the verb in brackets.

> As soon as I woke up I _____ (to think) it was going to be a good day. The sun was _____ (to shine) and the skies _____ (to be) blue. I _____ (to push) my covers to one side and _____ (to get) out of bed. When I _____ (to look) out of the window and _____ (to see) my friends I _____ (to know) I had been right.

Writing

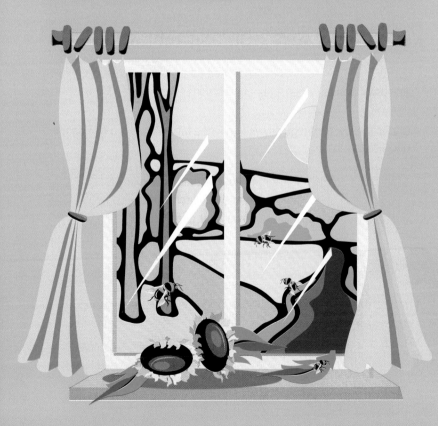

Check the facts

Here are some general rules about which kinds of writing require the use of which tense.

Type of writing	Tenses
Stories	can be written in the past, present or future tense or a mixture of all three. Most often, however, they are written in the past tense.
A **diary**	can also mix all three tenses with the focus on what has happened, how the writer now feels and the things that lie ahead.
A **newspaper report**	usually retells events that have happened and uses the past tense. However, a **report** which describes the way things are, such as a school report, is written in the present tense.
Explanations	of how something works are usually written in the present tense.
Instructions	on how to do something are usually written in the present tense.
A **discussion**	information presented from different viewpoints is usually written in the present tense.
A piece of **persuasive writing**	such as the text for an advertisement is usually written in the present tense.

• One of the few texts regularly written in the future tense is a **horoscope**. Why is this?

It is important in your writing that you:
• **know when to use which tense**
• **show control over your use of tense.**

Test yourself

1 Write a diary entry for today. Include reference to what you did this morning, what you're doing now and what you hope to do tomorrow.

Check that you have written in the past, the present and the future tenses.

Underline your use of verbs in the different tenses.

Check the facts

Some Year 9 pupils still use the same range of words in their writing that they used in primary school. Here is an example of such writing:

> I walk to school every morning. On the way I pass some different shops. There is a post office, a baker's and a newsagent's. Sometimes I stop and buy my breakfast in the baker's. Their jam doughnuts are really nice. Then I cross the road and call at my friend's house. He is usually not ready so I wait for him. Then we usually have to run the rest of the way so that we are not too late.

The writing is clear and accurate but the words used are fairly simple. Now read this redrafted version. As you read, underline words that demonstrate a wider vocabulary range.

> Every morning I walk reluctantly to school. On the way I pass a variety of shops which include a post office, a baker's and a newsagent's. Occasionally, I stop and buy my breakfast in the baker's. Their jam doughnuts are delicious and excellent value for money. My hunger satisfied, I cross the road and call at my friend's house. He is usually not ready so I wait for him. By the time he has gathered his numerous belongings together, we have no option but to run the rest of the way so as to avoid lateness and the detention that will inevitably accompany it.

Here the student uses a more mature range of words, for example, *variety, occasionally, numerous.*

> **The writing is more interesting and would gain a higher mark in an exam.**

Test yourself

1 Rewrite these sentences showing that you have a wide range of vocabulary. The first one has been done for you.
  a) He opened the parcel and looked inside.
     He tore open the tightly-wrapped parcel and gazed longingly at what lay inside.
  b) The classroom was quiet and the children were all sitting in rows.
  c) There was rubbish on the shelves and clothes on the floor.
  d) Having told her to go, he changed his mind and called her back.

Writing

BBC KS3 Check and Test: English

Check the facts

An adjective is a word that is used to tell the reader more about the noun.

An adjective can be placed before or after the noun, for example:

a <u>stunning</u> view	the view is <u>stunning</u>
a <u>naughty</u> child	the child is <u>naughty</u>
the <u>neglected</u> garden	the garden is <u>neglected</u>

Adjectives can be used to create a picture or image for the reader.

Think about how the adjectives in these three examples create different pictures of a smile.

a happy, cheerful smile

a tight, sarcastic smile

a sly, secretive smile

Now pick out the adjectives in this more detailed description of a face.

> The face was white and pinched, a startling contrast to the jet-black hair. The piercing blue eyes stared icily ahead, as a tight sarcastic smile developed slowly around the thin lips.

Think about how the adjectives are used. Can you picture this person?

Test yourself

1 Rewrite these phrases, placing the adjective(s) after the noun.
a bright and crisp morning   the calm sea
the dull and thundery sky

2 Think of a face that you know well. Write two or three sentences in which you describe it closely. Underline the adjectives in your description.

Check the facts

A verb is a word which is used to describe:

- **Actions and movements**, for example:
  She <u>jumped</u> off the horse and <u>fell</u> heavily.

- **Feelings and thoughts**, for example:
  Her leg <u>hurt</u> and she <u>suspected</u> it was broken.

- There are also parts of the verbs 'to have' and 'to be' which can be used on their own or with other verbs, for example:
  We <u>have</u> three pet snakes.   We <u>have bought</u> three pet snakes.
  They <u>are</u> at the shops.   They <u>are going</u> to the shops.

There is a huge range of verbs from which you can choose. Think, for example, of all the verbs that show how someone can move. Here are just a few of them. Can you think of more?

S/he ... jogged, marched, proceeded, travelled, bolted, zoomed, darted, dashed, streaked, ambled, strolled, lurched, glided, hurried, stampeded, hurtled, staggered, swayed, etc.

Aim to choose your verbs carefully so that they capture your ideas exactly.

Test yourself

1 List the verbs you can think of that show how someone can say something. Here are a few to start you off:
bellowed, screamed, shouted, whimpered, muttered

2 Rewrite these sentences using different combinations of verbs to create different effects.
a) The suspect turned and walked (dashed, hurtled, strolled) to the door.
b) The student moved (staggered, crept, darted) from his place and walked (stormed, rushed, drifted) out of the classroom.

Writing

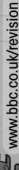

Writing

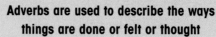

Check the facts

> **Adverbs are used to describe the ways things are done or felt or thought**

Some examples of adverbs are:
She jumped <u>carelessly</u> off the horse and fell <u>heavily</u>.
Her leg hurt <u>badly</u> and she <u>immediately</u> suspected it was broken.

Adverbs work with the verb. They answer questions about it, for example:

She jumped. How did she jump? She jumped carelessly.
She suspected. When did she suspect? She immediately suspected.

Many adverbs are formed by adding the suffix ly to the adjective, for example:

The girl was <u>careless</u> (adjective).   She jumped <u>carelessly</u> (adverb).
The fall was <u>heavy</u> (adjective).   She fell <u>heavily</u> (adverb).

> **You can improve your writing by choosing your adverbs carefully.**

Test yourself

1 Underline the adverbs in this passage. What questions do they answer?

> They stood impatiently outside the cinema, waiting for the doors to open. Suddenly the crowd surged forward. They showed their tickets and eventually found their seats.

2 Form adverbs from the following adjectives:

mysterious	thoughtful	happy	generous
rapid	angry	easy	wonderful

3 Write a description of a waterfall. Use adverbs to create a picture of how the waterfall sounds and moves.

Check the facts

The term imagery is applied to particular kinds of descriptive writing. Two forms of imagery often used by writers are similes and metaphors.

> **In a simile a writer compares one thing to another**

Here's an example of a simile:

> The diamond twinkled as brightly as sunshine on a brilliant summer's day.

The reader can picture sunshine on a brilliant summer's day and can use what they know about this to picture how brightly the diamond shone.
A simile is often introduced with the word *as* or *like*.

> **In a metaphor a writer says one thing actually is something else**

Here's an example of a metaphor:

> The lantern shone in the distance, a glittering star guiding her home.

Here the lantern is described as actually being a glittering star. The writer creates a mental picture of the lantern for the reader and also uses the image of the star to suggest the lantern is a guide.

Similes and metaphors have similar effects. They both help create a clearer picture of what is being described.

Test yourself

1 Copy and complete this chart. The questions will help you to identify how the writer uses simile and metaphor to create a picture for the reader.

Simile or metaphor	The picture it creates
The snow fell like confetti at a wedding.	What did it look like? How did it fall?
He spoke, his voice a slow beating on an African drum.	How did he speak? What did his voice sound like? Was it a friendly voice?

2 Create your own similes and metaphors to complete these sentences:
  a) The rain fell as   as
  b) The teacher spoke, her voice a
  c) The day was cold and miserable like a

Check the facts

Words can be used to create a particular atmosphere.

Compare the following passages and identify which passage you would expect to find in:

- a ghost story
- story about a family holiday
- a horror story.

What atmosphere is created in each passage?

A The drive stretched invitingly into the distance. At its end lay the cosy cottage, gleaming white in the winter sunshine, a trail of smoke puffing cheerily from the chimney revealing the warm welcome that lay ahead.

B The drive stretched threateningly into the distance. At its end stood the infamous cottage, blackened and sinister in the dark light of winter. A thin trail of smoke from the chimney only served to remind us of the danger that lay ahead.

C The drive stretched mysteriously into the distance. At its end, shrouded in mist lay the cottage. A wispy trail of smoke seeped from its chimney. But for that, all else was still and silent.

Notice how words are used to create the atmosphere:

- Different adverbs describe how the drive stretched into the distance: *invitingly, threateningly, mysteriously.*

- The cottage is: *gleaming white in the winter sunshine, blackened and sinister, shrouded in mist.*

What other differences in the use of words can you identify?

Aim to use words in your own writing to create a particular atmosphere.

Test yourself

1 This passage was written to describe a family holiday. Rewrite it as it might be written for either a ghost or a horror story.

It was almost light and we were racing along the lane to reach the farm before milking started. As we ran we could hear the sounds of morning all around us. The birds were singing cheerily and the gentle breeze was rustling noisily through the grass as though to wake the wildlife sleeping there.

Check the facts

Writers sometimes want their readers to feel a particular emotion. To achieve this they use words or phrases that **target particular emotions.** Read these examples. What feelings do you think the writers want their readers to feel? Match each example to the list below.

A Rotting corpses line the streets as war rages.

B Danger lurks on every corner until this evil killer is found.

C Many old, frail and helpless people face lonely and painful deaths.

D Are you doing your bit? For just £2.00 a week you could save lives.

pity	guilt	horror	fear

Were you right?

Example **A** aims to make the reader feel horror by referring to the bodies as *rotting corpses.*

Example **B** aims to make the reader feel fear by suggesting there is danger on *every corner.* The word *lurks* suggests it's something bad.

Example **C** aims to make the reader feel pity. The words *frail, helpless, lonely* and *painful* are chosen to help create this.

Example **D** aims to make the reader feel guilt. It uses a direct question and emphasises what could be achieved for a small amount of money.

> **When language is used to target emotions it's called emotive use of language.**

Test yourself

List five phrases you could use to make your reader feel pity for neglected animals. Here is an example: *living in appalling conditions.*

List five phrases you could use to make your reader feel anger that a motorway is to be built through their area. Here is an example: *imagine the toxic fumes.*

Check the facts

> One good way of developing your range
> of words is to use a **thesaurus.**

A thesaurus helps you to find and use:
- words you may not already know
- alternative words to the ones you use often.

It groups together words with similar meaning. The word you look up, or headword, is printed first in a larger font. Words that have a similar meaning to the headword are then listed in alphabetical order.

> Read this thesaurus entry for the word sad: *a sad expression, a sad story, etc.*
>
> careworn, cheerless, crestfallen, dejected, depressed, desolate, despairing, desperate, despondent, disappointed, disconsolate, discontented, discouraged, disgruntled, dismal, dissatisfied, distressed, doleful, down, downcast, down-hearted, dreary, forlorn, gloomy, glum, grave, grieving, grim, guilty, heart-broken, heavy, hopeless, joyless, low, lugubrious, melancholy, miserable, moping, morbid, morose, mournful, pathetic, penitent, pessimistic, pitiful, plaintive, regretful, rueful, sombre, sorrowful, sorry, tearful,
>
>  touching, tragic, troubled, unhappy, wistful, woeful, wretched.
>
> from *The Oxford Children's Thesaurus,*
> by permission of Oxford University Press

As you can see, **the thesaurus gives you a range of options for alternative words.** They wouldn't all be suitable for what you want to say, but some would.

Test yourself

1 Replace the word sad in these sentences with an effective substitute:
  a) The child was sitting with a sad and bored expression on her face.
  b) It is sad that you're not able to visit them.
  c) The teacher read a very sad story to the class.

2 Use a thesaurus to find alternative words for:

  mix   cruel   good   talk   quick

Check the facts

> **The purpose of a piece of writing is the reason for which it has been written.**

For example, a letter to a friend might be written to inform the reader of things that have happened. A recipe is usually written to instruct the reader on how to make something. Stories are often written to entertain the reader.

Read this text. What is it trying to do?

Spy Kids (PG)
(Robert Rodriguez, 2001, US)
Antonio Banderas, Carla Gugino, Alan Cumming, Teri Hatcher, 88 mins.
The man behind El Mariachi and Desperado makes one for the kids. Parents will thank him for creating a wild flight of the imagination - about a family of spies - that is as smart as his earlier, more bloodthirsty films.

from *The Guide, Guardian*

Were you right? This text is a review of a film. It aims to give the reader an idea of what the film is like.

A piece of writing can have more than one purpose. For example, the purposes of an advertisement can be:

- to inform the reader about a product
- to persuade the reader to buy it.

When starting a writing task, the first thing you need to work out is your purpose. Why are you writing? What are you hoping to achieve?

Test yourself

Read these questions, based on Key Stage 3 test questions. For each one, work out and write down the *purpose* or *purposes*.

a) Imagine you are a director of a new museum. Write a letter to headteachers of schools in the area encouraging then to bring groups of pupils to visit the museum.

b) Imagine you have been given a chance to talk in a year assembly. Choose an issue you feel strongly about. Write your speech trying to persuade other people to support your views.

Check the facts

The audience of a piece of writing is the intended reader.

The intended audience may be one person, as in a letter to a friend, or many people, as in a letter to a newspaper.

When you read a text, there are clues to help you identify the intended audience. Complete this chart by:
- working out the intended audiences of the following texts
- identifying the clues that helped you to decide.

The first one has been done for you.

Text	Intended audience(s)	Clues
A	Young children	Short sentences, simple words
B		
C		

Text A:

Two sets of teeth
Your first set of teeth are called milk teeth because they grow when you are a baby. There are 20 of these.

There are 32 teeth in a full adult set. Nobody really knows why people grow two sets of teeth.

from *What's Inside You?* by S. Mayes

Text B:

ORANGE-PINEAPPLE CHICKEN

1 x 1¼ kg (3 lb) chicken, quartered
salt
freshly ground white pepper
2 tablespoons vegetable oil
25 g (1 oz) butter
175 ml (6 fl oz) orange juice
2 x 225 g (8 oz) cans pineapple chunks, the juice reserved
(recipe needs 250 ml/8 fl oz)
extra pineapple juice, if necessary
3 lemon slices
50 g (2 oz) skinned almonds, toasted
sprigs flat leaf parsley, to garnish

PREPARATION TIME: 10 minutes
COOKING TIME: 1 hour
OVEN: 180°C, 350°F, Gas Mark 4

from *Cooking in a Casserole* by Yvette Stachowiack and Katherine Blakemore

www.bbc.co.uk/revision

Text C:

Hi Janie, How you doin'? Is the new place as bad as you expected? I've really missed you. Loads of things have been happening here...

When starting a writing task, **you need to identify your intended audience.** Who are you writing for? How will your audience affect the way you write?

Test yourself

Using the same questions, based on Key Stage 3 test questions, as in Unit 21, work out and write down the intended *audience* of each one.

a) Imagine you are a director of a new museum. Write a letter to headteachers of schools in the area encouraging them to bring groups of pupils to visit the museum.

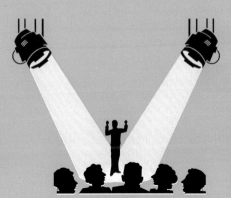

b) Imagine you have been given a chance to talk in a year assembly. Choose an issue you feel strongly about. Write your speech trying to persuade other people to support your views.

Check the facts

> Hi ya Baz.

> Hello, Sir.

You usually adapt the way you speak according to your purpose and audience. Students tend not to speak to their friends in the same way as they speak to their teachers. The language of the playground is usually **informal**. The language of the classroom is usually more **formal**.

It's the same with writing.

> **The way you write depends on your intended purpose and audience.**

Text A is an extract from an informal letter. **Text B** is an extract from a formal letter. The main features of each are highlighted for you.

Text A

Hi Steph,

How's it goin in the sunshine? Saw a brill concert last night — you'd've loved it! Haz and I nicked out early and zoomed back to her place to get changed. Nearly got grassed on by Sammy!...

- endings are left off words
- words are shortened
- slang is used
- punctuation is sometimes more varied

Text B

Dear Mr Clarke,

I wish to be considered for a work experience placement with your company. I am a student at St Paul's High School and am currently in Year 10. Having taken Geography and Art as my option subjects, I am going to...

- full name is used
- formal expression of ideas
- the endings of words are not cut
- words are not shortened

Test yourself

Write two messages.

1 To invite a friend to a sleepover, giving details of time and date. Use language informally.

2 To explain to a teacher why you can no longer attend a sporting event on Saturday morning. Use language formally.

Writing

www.bbc.co.uk/revision

30

Check the facts

In writing, words are organised into sentences and sentences are organised into paragraphs.

In hand-written texts, a paragraph is usually marked by the beginning of a new line and the indentation of the first word.

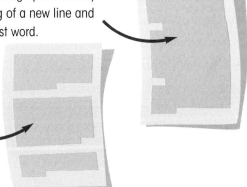

In printed texts, a new paragraph may be indicated by double spacing.

Paragraphs help the reader to follow the text more easily.

> **A new paragraph lets the reader know that the writer has moved the subject on in some way.**

For example, if you were writing a description of where you live you might decide to organise your writing in this way:

Paragraph 1 – the town/area in which I live

Paragraph 2 – the street in which I live

Paragraph 3 – my house

Paragraph 4 – the room in which I spend most of my time.

> **Use paragraphs to guide your reader through your writing and to get your ideas across more effectively.**

Test yourself

Here are some writing tasks you worked on in Units 21 and 22. Make paragraph plans for each of them.

  a) Imagine you are a director of a new museum. Write a letter to headteachers of schools in the area encouraging them to bring groups of pupils to visit the museum.
  b) Imagine you have been given a chance to talk in a year assembly. Choose an issue you feel strongly about. Write your speech trying to persuade other people to support your views.

Writing

BBC KS3 Check and Test: English

Check the facts

To paragraph effectively you need to:

- organise your material
- make fluent links from one sentence to another
- make fluent links from one paragraph to another.

Read this opening paragraph. Notice how:

- the subject is stated clearly in the opening sentence
- the sentences are linked by reference to the place.

> <u>There is a place</u> I particularly like to go to when I want some peace and quiet. <u>It is</u> about five miles from where I live, just a bus ride away, and is by the sea. Whenever I decide to go <u>there</u>, the day follows a familiar pattern.

The next three paragraphs have been mixed up. Place them in the correct order. Explain how you decided on the correct order.

> Just below the cliff-top lies a series of narrow, winding steps, which descend steeply to the shore. I negotiate these cautiously, for fear of breaking my ankle. The last thing I want is to be stranded half-way down a cliff.
>
> Finally, I arrive at the bottom. It is then that I heave a sigh of relief, drop my bag to the ground and collapse exhausted on the soft, golden sand.
>
> Firstly, I leave my house at about ten o'clock, just in time to catch the number 45 bus which deposits me, almost twenty minutes later, at the cliff-tops. From here the view is tremendous. You can see right across the bay and can spot, in the distance, trawlers and tankers headed for distant places.

Reread the three paragraphs. For each one work out how the sentences are linked.

Test yourself

Write four paragraphs about a place you like to go to. Aim to make fluent links within and between paragraphs. Use the example above as a model.

Check the facts

When writing you can write in:

• The **first person** – singular: **I**; plural: **we**

The first person is often used for autobiography, for example:

> As soon as I entered my house by the back door, my happiness started to seep away. Cook and Ah Sun were in the kitchen cleaning a fish for dinner. They hardly looked up when I walked by. I greeted them with the news that I was now the newly elected president of my class.
>
> from *Chinese Cinderella* by Adeline Yen Mah

• The **second person** – singular: **you**; plural: **you**

This is the least-used form. It is sometimes found in advice or instructions:

> # VIRGO
> **August 23 to September 22**
> **WEEK 1 Feb 1-7**
>
> With your ruler, Mercury, in your opposite sign for most of the week, your close relationships are all well-starred. So if there are problems to resolve (and it seems there are), deal with them now. Sticking your head in the sand won't help you or anyone else, and, with the stars all in your favour, you don't need to!
>
> from *Sugar* magazine March 2001

• The **third person** - singular: **he**, **she**, **it**; plural: **they**

The third person is often used in stories, for example:

> Of course his sisters sometimes called him a pest and told him to go away, but mostly the family included him in whatever they were doing and sometimes, not just on his birthday, did something they thought would amuse him. But even those times, Derek knew in his heart that he wasn't really meant to be there.
>
> from 'The Spring' by Peter Dickinson, from *Beware! Beware!*
> ed. by Jean Richardson

Test yourself

Write the opening sentences for a ghost story in:

  a) the first person   b)   the third person.

Check the facts

In your exam, you might be asked to *write about a real or imagined event*. This means that you can choose to:

- write about something that has actually happened
- use your imagination to create something entirely new.

> **Writing based on the imagination is called fiction.**

Many of the features of writing based on the imagination are the same as writing based on real events. You still need to:

- use a range of vocabulary
- order words clearly within sentences
- vary your use of sentence structures
- take care with handwriting, spelling and punctuation.

One of the best starting points when thinking about what makes writing based on the imagination different is to **draw on your own experience of good fiction**. Think about the types of things you like to read now and how your reading habits have changed since Year 7. What is it that makes you start a particular book and then continue to read it? Which writers have been most successful in drawing you into their imagined worlds?

Test yourself

Choose two fiction stories, long or short, that you have read in the last year. For each one list details about:

a) Where the stories took place

b) The main people in the stories and what you learned about them

c) The ways the stories started and ended

d) The things you enjoyed most about them.

Once you have identified some of the features of stories you have enjoyed reading, you can start to use these features in your own writing.

www.bbc.co.uk/revision

Writing

Check the facts

> Writers of stories often create an environment in which their stories take place. This may be based on a real or imagined place.

It may include details about:

- the place itself
- the weather
- the period of time in which the story takes place
- the society of the time.

This environment is called the **setting**.

This passage is from the opening of a short story. As you read it focus on what you learn about the setting.

> Paolo Saverini's widow lived alone with her son in a tiny cottage on the ramparts of Bonifacio. The town, built on a mountain spur, in some places actually overhanging the sea, faces the low-lying coast of Sardinia across the strait with its bristling reefs. At its foot on the other side it is almost entirely enclosed by a gash in the cliff like a gigantic passage, which serves as its harbour. The little Italian or Sardinian fishing-boats and once a fortnight the old puffing steamer, which runs to and from Ajaccio, come up as far as the first houses, after threading their way between two precipitous walls of rock.
>
> from *A Vendetta* by Guy de Maupassant

Test yourself

1 Make a list of all the different things you learn about the setting from the paragraph above.

2 Write your own opening paragraph to a short story. Focus on creating a clear setting in which the story can take place.

Writing

BBC KS3 Check and Test: English

Check the facts

Most stories are based on one or more central characters. Writers reveal their characters to their readers through:

Their appearance:

A tall woman with red hair stepped out of the passenger side.... She wore a black cowboy hat and black cowboy boots which were studded with turquoise stones. The sleeves on her shirt were rolled up, and her arms were covered with freckles, as was her face.

Their words:

"You sure he has no family?" the Warden asked Mr Pendanski.

"He had nobody," said Mr. Pendanski. "He was nobody."

The Warden thought for a moment. "Okay, I want you to destroy all of his records."

Mr. Pendanski nodded.

"He was never here," said the Warden.

Their actions:

The Warden turned to face Mr Sir, who was sitting on the fireplace hearth. She stepped toward him and struck him across the face.

Mr Sir stared at her. He had three long red marks slanting across the left side of his face. Stanley didn't know if the redness was caused by her nail polish or his blood.

It took a moment for the venom to sink in.

all three extracts from *Holes* by Louis Sachar

What things do you learn about the Warden from each of these extracts?

Test yourself

Create your own character. Follow these stages:

a) Decide what he or she looks like. What style of clothes? Any distinguishing features, such as freckles?

b) What kind of person is your character? What would he or she say? How would he or she say them?

c) How could you show what he or she is like through actions? How would he or she behave when angry?

Check the facts

The structure of a story refers to the way it's put together.

There are many different ways of structuring a story. Here are a few of them:

The linear method:

This follows the order of events as they happen. This is sometimes called the chronological order. The writer starts at the beginning and ends at the end. This is one of the most common methods of structuring a story.

Flashbacks:

The story does not follow a chronological order. The ending of the story is often placed at the beginning and the writer describes the events leading up to this by a series of flashbacks or recalled memories. This allows the writer to move easily between the past and the present. It is a useful way of introducing things that have happened a long time ago.

The twist in the tail:

The ending of the story is unexpected. The writer deliberately misleads the reader and then creates a surprise at the end. When the reader looks back he or she can find the clues that had been overlooked. This technique is often used in ghost and mystery stories.

When writing imaginatively in your exam, it's important to think carefully about how to structure your ideas.

You should aim to have an **impact** on your reader.

Test yourself

Read this recent exam task.

Write about an incident in which you had to leave a place you knew well. You could write about a real or an imaginary experience.

Plan the outline of an answer on this, using one of the methods described above.

Writing

BBC KS3 Check and Test: English

Check the facts

Your examiner will be marking many answers on the same task. Many of them will be very similar. To make an impression you need to do something different. One of the best ways of achieving something different is through the way you structure your ideas.

> **The more you experiment now, the easier it will be when it comes to your exam.**

Here are some more ways for you to try.

The diary form:

This allows the reader to get a very clear picture of the main character, the diary writer. Always in the first person, it's a way of presenting very personal thoughts and feelings. It also allows the writer to use an informal style of writing. Sometimes the diary form can be used as part of a longer story.

The dual narrator:

Two characters are used to tell the same story from different viewpoints, for example, a girlfriend and boyfriend or a parent and child. The writer may move several times from one character to another or allow one character to tell the whole story before moving to the other character. This technique allows the writer to show different attitudes and is an interesting way of exploring conflict.

Test yourself

Think again about this recent exam task.

Write about an incident in which you had to leave a place you knew well. You could write about a real or an imaginary experience.

Write diary entries to capture your thoughts and feelings on:

- the day you discovered you would have to leave the place
- two days before leaving when you said goodbye to friends
- the day itself
- two weeks later.

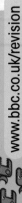

38

Check the facts

When you write to inform your aim is to tell your reader about something or somebody.

Writing that informs can be based entirely on known **facts** as in an encyclopedia:

> **Yeti**: A supposed ape-like creature said to live at the edge of the snow-line in high valleys of the Himalayan Mts; generally described as large, covered in brown hair, and walking upright like a human; first reported in 1889; foot-prints of length 15-30cm/6-12in have been photographed, but various expeditions have failed to find it; also known as abominable snowman.
>
> *from The Cambridge Encyclopedia ed. by David Crystal*

It may also include **opinion** as in this example:

> Have you ever seen a yeti? It's unlikely that you have unless you've travelled to the distant Himalayan Mountains and been one of the very few people fortunate enough to have sighted one of these rare creatures. Unfairly named the abominable snowman, the yeti is a large, brown-haired, ape-like creature who seems to avoid the company of man.

To make your informative writing interesting, aim to:

- use questions to draw your reader in
- relate the information to your reader
- give an appropriate amount of detail.

Test yourself

Choose an animal. Write two short informative accounts of it:
  a) using facts only
  b) using a mix of fact and opinion.

Check the facts

> When you write to explain, your aim is to make something clear to your reader. Explanation often answers the questions: What? How? Why?

An explanation usually follows a clear set of logical steps.

It may be an explanation of a **particular process**:

> To understand how volcanoes work, we need to take an imaginary journey to the centre of our planet. The Earth's centre, or core, is about 3,470km (2,156 miles) thick. It is made up of an inner layer of solid iron and an outer layer of molten iron, cobalt and nickel. Above the core lies about 2,900 km (1,802 miles) of mantle, made up of many different metals. The lower part of this layer is soft and oozy. The upper mantle is solid, but with pockets of hot, molten rock...
>
> from *Volcanoes* by Philip Steele

It may be an explanation of **a personal experience or feeling**:

> There were several reasons why I decided to go to Italy for my holidays. Firstly, I was drawn by the promise of endless blue skies and warm sunshine. I was tired of grey skies and grey days. Then there was the thought of delicious pizza and ice-cream, both top of my favourite foods list. Finally, there was the attraction of all those marvellous places I had read about... Venice, Rome, Florence... the list was endless.

Ideas are often linked by connectives in explanations. Here are some commonly used connectives:

Firstly...   Then...   Because...

As a result of...   Finally...   So...

Test yourself

Write a paragraph in which you explain how you met your best friend.
Aim to:
• organise your ideas in a logical order
• use some of the listed connectives to link your ideas.

Check the facts

When you write to describe you are trying to paint a picture with words. Your aim is to give your reader as clear a picture as you can.

It might be of a place:

drab

littering

> The house – the bit I'd seen so far – was really grotty. Not dirty, I don't mean that. I'm talking about dark paintwork, drab wallpaper and out-of-date fittings. There were no houseplants or flowers and yet there was an impression of clutter, of things chosen without care, crammed in corners and littering every surface.

Notice the amount of detail given here. How many things do you learn about the house? This **detail** is a feature of writing to describe.

Your description might be of a person:

> I looked at the kid and it was like I saw him for the very first time as a kid. He wasn't the monster I'd once believed him to be, and he wasn't the nuisance I'd been saddled with. He was neither a chore nor a shameful secret; he was a child: a frail, beautiful, grey-eyed child who should be out in the sunshine with other six-year-olds, not cooped up and mucked out and fed through bars like a battery hen.
>
> both extracts from *Abomination* by Robert Swindells

Notice:

- the use of **adjectives** to describe: a <u>frail</u>, <u>beautiful</u>, <u>grey-eyed</u> child
- the use of a **simile**: not cooped up and mucked out and fed through bars <u>like a battery hen</u>

These are both features of writing to describe.

Test yourself

Write a paragraph in which you describe either a place or a person. Aim to:

- give detail
- use adjectives
- use a simile.

Writing

BBC KS3 Check and Test: English

Check the facts

In your exam, you might be asked to describe an event. You need to give your reader a clear picture of what happens and the way it happens. One way to do this is to **use verbs effectively**. Read this passage. Some of the verbs used to describe the event are underlined for you. As you read, underline other verbs which you think help to create a clear picture.

Father <u>growled</u> an oath and there were sounds of a scuffle. Mother began to <u>wail</u>. I <u>turned</u>, <u>scooped</u> the kid out of the playpen and <u>started</u> up the steps. He was light. Almost weightless. Father was at the top with his back to me and his arms spread, <u>blocking</u> my progress and my sister's view but the end was in sight and nothing was going to stop me finishing it now. *Nothing.* I twisted sideways and rammed my shoulder into the small of his back. He didn't move much, but the woman got a glimpse of her child and that was enough. She flung Mother from her, side-stepped Father, snatched the kid out of my arms, and half-ran towards the open door. The child covered his eyes with his hands and began to scream. It was the light streaming through the doorway. The sunlight. He'd never encountered such brightness. It seared him.

from *Abomination* by Robert Swindells

Aim to use a range of verbs of action in your own writing when describing a particular event.

Test yourself

Write a paragraph describing an incident of bullying. Aim to use verbs effectively.

Here are some verbs you could use:

scream, tear, rip, punch, threaten, shout, shudder, cry, abuse, retreat, torment, pinch, injure, shove, twisted, rammed, move, flung, side-stepped, snatched, half-ran, covered, scream, streaming, encountered, seared

Check the facts

> **When you write to persuade, you are trying to make your reader do something or believe something.**

This type of writing is often used in:

- **advertisements**, where the writer is trying to persuade you to buy a particular product
- **charity appeals**, where the writer is trying to persuade you to give your support.

Read this extract from a holiday brochure carefully. Some of the more commonly-used features of writing to persuade have been highlighted for you.

adjectives used to create a positive impression		alliteration used for effect

It's all here - glorious sunshine, beautiful beaches and a vibrant, bubbly resort bursting with fun and good humour.

The sun seems to shine permanently onto the white sands of the Costa Blanca. Benidorm is particularly fortunate that the main sweep of its beaches faces south, catching the rays as long as the sun shines – and in this part of Spain that's almost all day every day! Benidorm takes looking after holidaymakers very seriously! The miles of soft sand, shelving gently into the warm waters of the Mediterranean are ideal for children, but if they fancy a change of scenery why not try the Aquapark nearby?

from *Thomson's Summer Sun 2001*

exaggeration for effect	exclamation for effect	rhetorical question used to draw reader in

Test yourself

Write a short extract for a holiday brochure on a place you know well. It could be your home town. You should aim to:

- write about 100 words
- use adjectives to create a positive impression
- use alliteration, exaggeration and exclamation for effect
- use rhetorical questions to draw the reader in.

Writing

BBC KS3 Check and Test: English

Check the facts

When you write to argue, your aim is to present and develop a particular point of view.

Start with **a statement of the subject and the main issues** surrounding it:

> The question of school uniform is one that arouses strong feelings. On the one side are the parents and teachers who argue that it looks tidy and helps to keep good discipline in schools. On the other hand are the students who want to have some choice in what they wear and express their individuality through their clothes.

look closely at **the arguments 'for'** and **give supporting evidence**:

> The price of a school uniform is a relevant factor. It is often cheaper to buy a uniform which is worn daily than to have to clothe a child in the latest fashions which cost a fortune and become dated very quickly...

Next look closely at **arguments 'against'** and **give supporting evidence**:

> Teachers argue that students will look scruffy and untidy in their own clothes but on non-uniform days teachers always comment on how nice everyone looks in their own clothes...

End with a conclusion, clearly stating **your own point of view**, for example:

> As long as students take reasonable care with their appearance, I can't see why they should have to wear a uniform. Most parents and most teachers don't so why should we?

Test yourself

Argue the case either 'for' or 'against' compulsory homework:
- Start with a statement of the subject and the main issues.
- Look at the arguments 'for' and give supporting evidence.
- Look at the arguments 'against' and give supporting evidence.
- End with a conclusion stating your own point of view.

Writing

Check the facts

When you write to advise, you're trying to help your reader. You find this type of writing in **magazines**, **newspapers** and school **textbooks**.

> **The aim is to get the reader on your side so that he or she is prepared to listen to the advice you have to offer.**

Read this extract from a magazine problem page. Some of the more commonly used features of writing to advise have been highlighted for you.

Q My boyfriend's the best thing that's ever happened to me, but I don't feel as if I'm good enough for him...

A It sounds like you're a great person, Nikki, whose self-confidence is a bit deflated at the moment. Don't worry - most of us go through this at some stage. Often, when we fall for someone, we're so in awe of them that we forget our own great qualities. In this case, your boyfriend can see how special you are but, unfortunately, you can't.

Try this simple routine to boost your confidence – each morning, look in the mirror and tell yourself that you're attractive and your guy is just as lucky to have you as you are to have him. Hopefully, you'll soon start to feel more positive about yourself – and your relationship.

from Sugar magazine March 2001

- addresses reader directly
- offers reassurance
- use of third person plural suggests a shared problem
- use of present tense
- try, look, tell – use of directives
- offers suggestion for dealing with problem

Writing

Test yourself

Write the reply to this problem. Remember to:

- address your reader directly
- reassure your reader
- offer suggestions for dealing with the problem.
- use the present tense
- show understanding

Q I've got lots of spots and I've tried everything to get rid of them. Some products worked at first but not anymore. I lead a healthy lifestyle with lots of exercise but I still get bad skin. Please help.

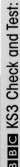

Check the facts

> When you write to analyse, your aim is to examine a particular topic closely.

You could be writing an analysis of a poem or of the results of an experiment. Writing to analyse sometimes involves explanation of how and why things happen.

The language of analysis is usually:
- very precise
- formal and impersonal
- reliant on technical terms.

Read the following analysis of these famous lines from Macbeth.

use of technical terms

evidence

> **Is this a dagger which I see before me,**
> **The handle toward my hand?**   (Act II, scene i)

These are the opening lines of a very famous soliloquy, in which Shakespeare reveals Macbeth's innermost thoughts to the audience. At this stage in the play Macbeth is already resolved to kill King Duncan, having 'settled' on the matter at the end of the previous scene. It would seem that the dagger is both a symbol of his evil thoughts and a physical representation of them. The handle is pointed towards his hand, suggesting that it is inviting him to take hold of it.

precise detail

formal and impersonal tone

The annotations that surround the text highlight some of the features of writing to analyse. Analysis is also often associated with **facts and figures**.

Test yourself

Choose four lines from the Shakespeare play that you're studying for your National Tests. Write a close analysis of these four lines. Base your writing on the model above. Aim to:
- use technical terms
- adopt a formal and impersonal tone
- give precise detail
- refer to evidence in the text.

Check the facts

> **When you write to review, your aim is to assess something for your reader.**

You might, for example, be asked to write a review of a **book**, **play** or **film**.

A review usually:
- has a brief summary of at least part of the plot
- hints at parts of the plot not included in the summary
- makes relevant comments on the subject
- gives an assessment or recommendation
- is written in the present tense.

How many of these features can you identify in this book review?

Big City Eyes by Delia Ephron

Divorcee Lily moves out of Manhattan to the Long Island coast with her teenage son Sam to save him from the big, bad city and improve their relationship. At sleepy Sakonnet Bay, she lands a job as a columnist for the local newspaper and Sam enrols in high school.

Somewhat predictably, life in a small community turns out to be just as turbulent and weird as life in the city. Lily starts an affair with a local cop and Sam falls in love with Deirdre, an androgynous classmate who will only speak Klingon (the only truly comic bit of the book). Lily and the cop stumble across a naked woman who later turns up murdered, but this never takes off as a sub-plot. Lily and Sam's relationship doesn't improve much either.

This is a book with nothing much to say – a disappointment after Ephron's promising fictional debut, Hanging Up. She is better known as a screenwriter – and this possibly would have been a better movie.

from the *Daily Mail*, 20 April 2001

Test yourself

Write a review of either a book or a film.
- it should be about 150 words
- include the features of a review listed at the start of this unit
- remember to write in the present tense.

Check the facts

> When you comment on something,
> you're giving your opinion on it.

'I find this play difficult to understand,' is an opinion and a simple comment. In your English writing, however, you need to develop your comments further.

Here is an example of a question where you're asked to comment.

> *Look at the last paragraph of the article.*
> *How effective do you think this paragraph is as an ending for the article?*

In your answer you should comment on:

• the way it links with the heading, the opening paragraph and the rest of the article

• the way in which it's written and how this is different from the rest of the article.

Refer to words and phrases in the article to support your ideas.

As you can see, your examiner is looking for your ability to:

• form an opinion

• give reasons for your opinions

• refer to the text to support your opinions

• show, through your comments, that you have thought carefully about the text and the question.

Some useful words and phrases to use when writing to comment are:

It seems that...	This gives the impression of...
This suggests that...	The effect of this is...
I think...	An alternative view would be...
Because of this...	This is evident in...

Test yourself

Choose a subject that has recently made the news headlines and in which you're interested, for example global warming. Comment on:

• the impact this subject has on your life

• the way the subject has been covered in the news.

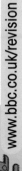
Writing

Check the facts

In your exam, you may be asked to write a letter.

There are two types of letter – formal and informal.

The following outline shows you how to set out a formal letter. The recipient is the person to whom you're writing.

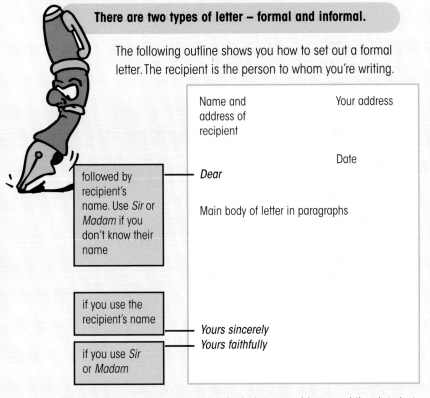

Name and address of recipient	Your address
	Date
Dear	
Main body of letter in paragraphs	
Yours sincerely	
Yours faithfully	

followed by recipient's name. Use *Sir* or *Madam* if you don't know their name

if you use the recipient's name

if you use *Sir* or *Madam*

In an informal letter you still need to include your address and the date but not name and address of the recipient. Use the recipient's first name or the name by which you usually call them, for example, *Dear John, Dear Gran.* End informally with *Love from* or something similar.

Sometimes, in the exam, you may be asked not to include the addresses. **Follow the instructions you're given carefully.**

Test yourself

Read the following questions based on recent exam tasks and then set out two letters in reply, using the correct form. You don't need to write the whole letter.

1 Your class has agreed to help a local children's hospital or home. Write a letter to the parents of your year group explaining what you plan to do.

2 Write a letter to a friend about an unusual event, explaining your thoughts and feelings about what happened.

43 More about letters

Check the facts

Getting the layout of your letter right is only a small part of the task.

> **It's what you say in your letter that's most important.**

Read the following letter carefully. The notes next to it give you some clues on how to write a good letter.

Writing

Dear Mr Sanders,

I recently read your letter in the local newspaper about your daughter, Jade, who had been seriously ill. You said that there was treatment available for her but that she needed to travel to America and that this would cost more than your family could afford. I hope I may be able to help.

> clear opening which identifies the issue

Two years ago my family was in a similar situation when my sister Zoe needed very expensive treatment. Thanks to our friends and neighbours we were able to raise the money for this and she is now well and full of life. I have an idea that, hopefully, will allow Jade to feel the same way.

> development of ideas

> written in the first person, using *I* and *we*

I have spoken with friends at school, and my form tutor, and we want to organise a sponsored overnight sports marathon to raise money for Jade's treatment. We hope to go ahead with this on Friday, 21st June and wondered if you would come and start our event off. My sister, Zoe, is also taking part.

> clear organised detail

I do hope you will be able to come. Together, I am sure we will get your daughter to America.

> emphasis of aim at end

Yours sincerely,

Tom Jordan

> ideas organised into paragraphs

Test yourself

Write a letter to a charity of your choice, explaining how you hope to raise money. Use the above letter as a model.

Check the facts

Articles usually appear in **newspapers** and **magazines**. They can be on almost **any subject**. Articles often combine **a range of different types of writing** including writing to inform, to describe, to advise, to argue and to persuade. Articles often contain some distinctive features. Look at the sample article below.

Dying for a drink?

> play on words which suggests that drinking can kill

How many times have you been drunk? Never? Once? Five times? More than twenty times? Chances are, you'll have been drunk at least once. According to a recent report, despite the fact that drinking under 18 is illegal, Britain's teenagers drink more frequently and from a younger age than teens in almost any other European country and the figures are rising all the time.

> rhetorical questions to make the reader think

> written in the present tense

Drinking to excess has been dubbed 'binge drinking' by the media, and has been defined as drinking more than seven units of alcohol in one drinking session for women and drinking ten units or more in one drinking session for men.

Drinking to excess

According to a recent World Health Organisation report:

> sub-heading used to summarise the content of each section

- A quarter of British teenagers questioned had been drunk 20 times or more.
- British teenagers were second (behind Danish teens) in the number of teenagers surveyed who had been drunk three times or more during the last 30 days.
- A third of English teens admit to drinking regularly.

> bullet points used to summarise factual evidence

'There are a range of problems associated with binge drinking' confirms Andrew McNeill, co-director of the Institute of Alcohol Studies. 'Some are medical – in rare cases binge drinking can actually kill you and persistent binge drinking as a teenager can lead to permanent brain damage because your brain is not fully developed.

> the views of an 'expert' are used

from *Sugar* magazine May 2001

> content is organised into paragraphs

While many articles are printed in columns, this is a word processing function and you do not need to do this in your exam.

Test yourself

Write the opening three paragraphs of an article for a teenage magazine on a subject that concerns you. Aim to use some of the features listed above.

Writing

BBC KS3 Check and Test: English

Check the facts

Speech writing is a very different form to a letter or article. For a start, **a speech is intended to be spoken, not read**. The aim is to have an impact on the listener. Here are some of the main features of effective speeches.

The speaker addresses the audience directly:
> I'd like you to imagine, just for a moment, how it must feel to be...

Ideas are grouped in sets of three for maximum effect:
> Consider the horror of watching a child drift away from you, the horror of not being able to help and, worst of all, the horror of watching that child die before your eyes.

Words are repeated for impact:
> This is the misery caused by drugs, a misery that we cannot allow to continue.

Exclamations and short sentences are used for impact:
> This cannot go on! The misery must be stopped!

Rhetorical questions are used to make the listener think:
> How much longer are we going to wait before the dealers are stopped?

The speaker uses the first person plural to involve the listener:
> Together, we can make a difference.

Test yourself

Complete this task. Aim to use some of the features of speeches listed above.

Imagine you have been given a chance to talk in a year assembly. Choose an issue you feel strongly about. Write your speech trying to persuade other people to support your views.

Check the facts

> The first few minutes of any writing task are probably the most important. It is then that you choose what you're going to write and how you're going to write it.

The first thing you need to do is to **choose your task** carefully. Be sure that:
- you understand what you're being asked to do
- you have good ideas to write about.

It's important to **break the task down** when you first read it. You can do this by asking some simple questions:
- What is my purpose?
- Who is my intended audience?
- What form should my writing take?

When breaking a question down, it often helps to **highlight** key words **and/or underline** phrases. Look at this writing task:

Write   an article for a travel magazine, describing   a place that is beautiful but mysterious.

In your writing you   could   :

• try to create the atmosphere of the place in your description

•   aim to persuade readers   that this place would be an interesting place to visit

Purpose: to describe a place that is beautiful but mysterious; to persuade readers to visit.

Intended audience: the readers of a travel magazine; the examiner.

Form: an article for a travel magazine.

Test yourself

Break these tasks down into purpose, intended audience and form.

1 Write a letter to a friend about an unusual event, explaining your thoughts and feelings about it. Use a real or made-up event.

2 Imagine you have been given a chance to talk in a year assembly. Choose an issue you feel strongly about. Write your speech trying to persuade other people to support your views.

BBC KS3 Check and Test: English

Writing

53

Check the facts

Once you have fully understood the task, you need to **gather a range of ideas**.

You can do this by **brainstorming** a series of questions connected to the task, for example:

Write a letter to a friend about an unusual event, explaining your thoughts and feelings about it. Use a real or made-up event.

Where did it happen?

What happened?

Who else is involved?

Unusual event

When?

What do I think now?

How do I feel?

Why do I feel this way?

Once you have gathered your ideas, you need to **plan the order** in which you're going to deal with your ideas. You could do this by:

- linking and numbering the different ideas in your brainstorm
- make a plan outlining briefly the contents of each paragraph.

Test yourself

Using the ideas above, make your own brainstorm and paragraph plan for this task.

Check the facts

The opening of any piece of writing is important. It is your chance to:
* capture your examiner's attention
* make a good first impression.

Here are some different ways of opening your writing. They are written in response to this task:

> *Write about an incident in which you had to leave a place you knew well.*

* **Rhetorical question:**
  Have you ever hated a place so much you wanted to destroy it?

The question immediately draws the reader in and makes him or her think.

* **Imperatives:**
  Check the windows. Close the door. Look back one last time.

The imperatives *check, close* and *look* address the reader directly and give the writing a dramatic start

* **Simile:**
  The dark inside this room was as black as the soul of a ruthless murderer.

The simile immediately creates an image in the mind of the reader.

* **Exclamation:**
  'Leave now and never come back!'

This gives the writing a dramatic opening and makes the reader want to read on.

The same techniques can be used to end your writing. **You want to leave your reader with a new idea or a distinct image or a question that they will need to think about.** Another useful technique for an ending is **aposiopesis**. This is when you create a sense that there's more to follow or that the reader must work out how the story ends. Here's an example:

> She turned to look at the place that had almost destroyed her. She would be back...

Test yourself

Think of three different openings and endings for this writing task. Aim to use some of the techniques listed above.

Describe a person you know who has influenced you or been very important in your life.

Writing

BBC KS3 Check and Test: English

55

49 Drafting and checking

Check the facts

Drafting

Writers often redraft their work many times to get it exactly right. They change words, sentences and whole paragraphs.

Read the following example carefully. It shows how a paragraph could be improved using simple redrafting techniques.

> close by
> I had lived in the same house since I was born. All my
> friends lived ~~around me~~ and we all went to the same school.
> ~~When~~ my parents told me we were going to move to a town
> dreary
> almost one hundred miles away I was ~~really cross~~.
> I can remember clearly the day   away. I   devastated

You can use some of these redrafting techniques in an exam.

Checking

Spend five minutes at the end of your exam checking your writing.

Use this time to make sure that:
- it makes clear sense
- the word endings are correct
- the punctuation is appropriate
- your spelling is accurate.

Here is an example of work that has been carefully checked:

> Carlie   arrived   home, I   couldn't
> Having ~~arived~~ at my new ~~home~~ I was filled with dread.
> My older sister ~~carlie~~ told me to cheer up but I ~~couldent~~.
> I ~~whent~~ to my new room and looked out of the window. There
> was nothing to ~~intrest~~ me ~~here~~ I could ~~of~~ cried.
> went   interest   here. I   have

Test yourself

Redraft and correct this paragraph:

> The first week dissappeared quiet quickly as there was so much to do. We had to unpack all the cases hang curtens and make the house as nice as we could. Then we had to start at our new school. Having left so many good friends behind I wasent looking forward to this bit at all.

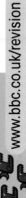

www.bbc.co.uk/revision

56

Check the facts

- **Arrive for your exam in good time.** Make sure you've had something to eat. Have a good pen and a spare.

- **Read the questions carefully.** Choose the one you can do best in the time you have.

- **Underline or highlight important words or phrases** in the question.

- **Identify the purpose, audience and form.**

- **Plan your ideas carefully.** You need to decide:
  - what you're going to say
  - the order in which you're going to say it
  - how you're going to say it.

- **Think about the tone of your writing.** Should it be formal or informal?

- Aim to **impress your examiner** by:
  - expressing your ideas clearly
  - using a range of sentence structures
  - using a range of vocabulary.

- Aim for a **high level of accuracy.** Think about:
  - paragraphing
  - punctuation
  - spelling.

- If you run short of time, make sure you **bring your writing to a proper ending** - even if it's not the one you had planned!

- Allow five minutes to **check your work carefully**.

Test yourself

Go through each of the above points carefully. Make sure you understand each point. If you don't, go back to the unit that dealt with it.

Check the facts

> Remember that scenes involving reports by minor characters can often contain information that is very important to the narrative of the play.

- When you look at Shakespeare plays, you need to be aware of **key points in the narrative**. Often, there are scenes and speeches where characters bring you up-to-date with events that you don't see on the stage.

- Remember that one great influence on Shakespeare was **Ancient Greek theatre**. In Ancient Greek plays, many events were reported to the audience by the characters. (See more about Ancient Greek theatre in Unit 53.)

- Look at **the Captain's speeches** in Act I scene ii of **Macbeth**. Here, he gives a report of the battle between the forces loyal to King Duncan and those of the rebel Macdonald and the Norwegian lord. In his report he:

  – tells of the ferocity of the battle

  – speaks highly of Macbeth.

The captain emphasises Macbeth's immense physical courage and his loyalty; this counterbalances your impression of Macbeth from his association with the witches in scene i.

Test yourself

Look at the speeches of the Old Man in Act II scene iv of *Macbeth*.

What do you find out about the state of Scotland after the murder of Duncan?

Check the facts

Important points in the narrative of Shakespeare's plays are often explained by quite minor characters for two main reasons:

- To move the story on and pick up the pace of the drama.
- To re-emphasise parts of the plot that have already been mentioned.

As an example, look at **the role of the Sea Captain** in Act I scene ii of *Twelfth Night*

- In Act I, you meet Orsino and are told by Valentine of Olivia's response to the death of her brother.

- Then, the **Sea Captain re-emphasises the vows** of Olivia so that the audience is quite clear about the difficulties faced by Orsino in his amorous pursuit of Olivia.

- He also **reports his sighting of Sebastian** at the time of the shipwreck, preparing you for Sebastian's later appearance and the confusion it causes in the latter stages of the play.

> **Always pay careful attention to things minor characters say. Try to work out what effect the information in their speeches is having on the course of the play.**

Test yourself

Look at Act III scene iii of *Twelfth Night*.

What do you find out about the intended actions of Antonio that will have a dramatic effect later in the play?

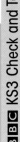

Shakespeare

BBC KS3 Check and Test: English

Shakespeare

Check the facts

You can also see Shakespeare's use of minor characters to move the story along or give the audience background information in this example from Act I scene ii of **Henry V**.

- **The French ambassador** outlines the history of diplomatic problems between the English and the French, including English claims to the French crown going back to Edward III.

- This lays the ground for Henry's strong-minded pursuit of French territory and his insulting gift of tennis balls.

- The scene also provides an opportunity for Henry to show that he's no longer a wild young man, but a mature and responsible monarch.

Shakespeare and Ancient Greek theatre

> **Shakespeare was greatly influenced by Ancient Greek theatre.**

- In Ancient Greek plays, many events, particularly those involving bloodshed and death, happened 'off-stage'.

- Greek playwrights often used the **device** of an actor or group of actors, who reported on events that happened off-stage. They were called the **Chorus**. The Chorus:

  – filled in narrative not shown on the stage

  – clarified actions

  – commented on characters.

In *Henry V*, there is a Chorus that sets the historical scene and reminds the audience that they will need to use their **imagination** to 'see' the great events not shown on stage.

Test yourself

Look at the speech of the Chorus in Act II, the Prologue, of *Henry V*.

What do you find out about the 'corrupted men' that has dramatic significance for the character of Henry soon afterwards?

Check the facts

Understanding characters through their actions

You will need to go into the exam with **ideas about the characters** in your chosen play. Remember that there are no right and wrong answers. All your ideas are acceptable as long as you can support them with references to the play.

> **Characters in a play reveal themselves to you in the same ways that real people do. One of the ways you get to know people is through their actions.**

Look at **Malvolio** in Act II scene v of *Twelfth Night* before he picks up the letter at line 81.

- His words and the actions that would go along with them on stage show what an insufferably **pompous** and **ambitious** character he is.

Having been three months married to her, sitting in my state ...

- He thinks aloud about how he would behave after his 'wedding' and is made a fool of by **witty** and **honest Maria**, much to the audience's enjoyment.

You don't need to be told by others about his character; his actions tell you all you need to know about him.

Test yourself

Choose one of the following scenes. Decide what you find out about the named character from their actions.

> **1** Henry with the conspirators in Act II scene ii, lines 40-76 of *Henry V*.
>
> **2** Lady Macbeth in Act II scene ii, lines 55-75 of *Macbeth*.
>
> **3** Sir Toby in Act III scene iv, lines 185-202 of *Twelfth Night*.

Shakespeare

Check the facts

Understanding characters by what's said about them

> Another way to develop ideas about characters is to listen to what is said about them by others whom you have come to see as reliable, or whom you know have a sound knowledge of the character in question.

Look at **what Olivia says about Orsino** in Act I scene v, lines 261-265 of *Twelfth Night*.

- It has already been established that Olivia is a serious person, who doesn't hand out praise lightly. Yet she paints an extremely flattering portrait of Orsino, pointing out his good looks, his wealth, his **sound reputation** and his **virtuous character**.

- You are left in no doubt that Orsino is a fine man; a 'good catch' for any woman. The fact that Olivia is not in love with him adds to the truthfulness of what she says. She has no emotional bias and can provide a reliable character report for the audience.

> *... of great estate, of fresh and stainless youth.*

- Your initial thoughts about the good character of Orsino are confirmed.

Test yourself

Choose one of the following scenes. Decide what you find out about a character from what is said by others.

1 Sir Toby from what Malvolio says in Act II scene iii, lines 84-97 of *Twelfth Night*.

2 Macduff from what Ross and Lady Macduff say in Act IV scene ii, lines 1-28 of *Macbeth*.

3 Henry from what Fluellen and Gower say in Act IV scene vii, lines 39-53 of *Henry V*.

Check the facts

Understanding characters by what is said by them

> Characters also reveal who they really are when they talk about themselves and their ideas.

In drama, revealing what a character's inner thoughts are often involves a **soliloquy** or an **aside**. The fact that the character is talking directly to the audience makes it sound as if you're hearing their genuine thoughts and feelings. This can certainly have a strong effect on your ideas about a character.

Look at **Macbeth's soliloquy** in Act I scene vii, lines 1-28 of *Macbeth*.

- He reveals his thoughts about the plan to murder Duncan.

- In the first ten lines he tells you that he would definitely go ahead if there were no consequences. From this, you learn that he's a person who **doesn't want to take responsibility** for his actions.

- Later, he mentions seven good reasons *not* to kill Duncan and then can only offer his own **unworthy ambition** as a counter argument. Since he does go ahead with the murder, what does this tell you about his character?

> *I have no spur to prick the sides of my intent, but only vaulting ambition.*

- It's difficult to see the act as anything other than the premeditated murder of a good and worthy king by an **irresponsible and selfish madman**.

Test yourself

Choose one of the following scenes. Decide what you find out about the character from what he or she says.

1 Macbeth in Act I scene iv, lines 48-53 of *Macbeth*.

2 Olivia in Act I scene v, lines 311-314 of *Twelfth Night*.

3 Henry in Act IV scene i, lines 226-236 of *Henry V*.

Shakespeare

BBC KS3 Check and Test: English

Check the facts

You need to think about relationships between characters.

One of the most common and yet most powerful relationships explored in Shakespeare's plays is the **love relationship**. Here's one example of the complexity of relationships and realistic depth of feeling that you can find in Shakespeare.

In **Twelfth Night**, **Viola** is interested in **Orsino** from the moment she meets him in Act I scene ii, lines 51-59.

- Viola then finds herself falling in love with Orsino. This is a major problem for Viola because the Duke thinks she's a young man.

- The Duke uses her as a messenger and she has to listen without comment to Olivia praising Orsino's character and appearance. Imagine how hard that must be to hear for someone who is in love with him herself.

- You know from Viola's aside to the audience in Act I scene iv that she wants to marry Orsino. Therefore, you can presume that her words of love to Olivia actually represent her feelings for Orsino.

- Viola's speech in Act I scene v, lines 271-279 expresses her depth of feeling. For Viola, love is a very intense emotion and not something to be trifled with. Her use of extreme language prepares you for later scenes as she tries to win her love.

Halloo your name to the reverberate hills

Test yourself

Find a section in your chosen play where one character declares love for another. Decide what **the language of the declaration** tells you about how they see the nature of love.

Check the facts

Characters in Shakespeare's plays may have a **dramatic relationship** not because of their love or respect for one another but **because of their opposition** to one another.

> **Opposition between characters can exist because of fundamental differences in their characters, or because of their contrasting reactions to circumstances.**

In *Twelfth Night*, Malvolio and Feste are opposites.

- **Feste** is employed in Olivia's house to provide **witty entertainment**, whilst **Malvolio** is the **serious-minded** head of the servants.

- Some of their differences can be seen in Act I scene v, where **Feste** engages in **amusing word-play** with Olivia over the death of her brother. Olivia is impressed with Feste's wit whilst **Malvolio**'s response is more **cynical and sarcastic**.

> Olivia:
> What kind of man is he?

> Malvolio:
> Why, of mankind

In *Macbeth*, conflict between Macbeth and **Banquo** develops because of circumstances in the play.

- At the beginning, they are both portrayed as brave and loyal, but they act very differently after the encounter with the witches.

- Ultimately, Macbeth orders the murder of Banquo as well as his son, Fleance. **Banquo's continuing loyalty** to Duncan is in dramatic opposition to **Macbeth's treachery**.

Test yourself

Choose two characters from your selected play who are opposite either in temperament or in their response to events around them.

Decide how this opposition **adds to the drama** of the play.

Shakespeare

BBC KS3 Check and Test: English

Shakespeare

Check the facts

Many of Shakespeare's plays feature characters from **wide-ranging social backgrounds**. You can tell a lot from how the different characters relate and behave towards each other.

> **The way that royalty and aristocrats interact with ordinary people is a good indicator of character.**

In Act IV scene iii of **Henry V**, the King addresses his troops before the battle of Agincourt.

- The speech indicates Henry's regard for his fellow countrymen – no matter what their background. He even offers to let them leave the battlefield, promising not to charge them with desertion, and to give them money for their journey home. This scene adds to the positive impression of Henry as **a King with a concern for his whole nation**, not just the nobility.

In **Twelfth Night**, **Olivia** is the lady of a great house and **Maria** is a servant. However, Olivia treats Maria more as a friend and relies on her sensible observations.

- This relationship helps you to see Olivia as a **more sensitive, feeling character**, in contrast to the rather austere picture you receive of her at the start of the play. It helps to prepare you for the dramatic changes in Olivia's behaviour, first with Viola and then with Sebastian, so that it doesn't seem as though it is completely out of character.

Test yourself

Find a scene, or part of a scene, in your chosen play where one of the high-born characters is talking to one of the common people or a servant.

What does the **language and attitude** of the higher-born person tell you about his or her character?

Check the facts

In your exam answer, you'll need to do more than write about the content of the scene, characters and relationships. You'll need to comment on how Shakespeare's language has an effect on the drama in the scene.

> **Shakespeare used language to produce convincing word-pictures that set the scene for the audience.**

- Remember that the playhouses of Shakespeare's time didn't have the **technology** for the **special effects** of today's theatres.

- The writer had to plant the scene clearly in the minds of the audience, using only words.

Look at Act II scene i of **Macbeth**. Shakespeare is setting the scene at midnight on a dark night. Banquo says:

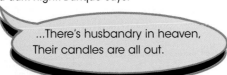

...There's husbandry in heaven, Their candles are all out.

- Banquo's words create a picture of the stars being put out the way a careful householder would put out all the lights before going to bed. This is a picture everyone can relate to.

- It also has a **strong dramatic effect**. The black night is the setting for dark deeds – the killing of Duncan, which is central to the drama.

The audience of Shakespeare's time would have recognised this dramatic use of the setting and would have known that something fearful was going to happen. This may not be so natural for the modern audience, but you need to look out for this sort of scene- and atmosphere-setting in Shakespeare's plays.

Test yourself

Choose one of the following scenes and decide how the language helps to create the setting for the audience.

1 Act IV scene ii, lines 41-50 of *Twelfth Night*.

2 Act III scene v, lines 14-31 of *Macbeth*.

3 Act III scene i, lines 3-17 of *Henry V*.

Shakespeare

BBC KS3 Check and Test: English

Shakespeare

Check the facts

Shakespeare's language often describes incidents that have not happened on stage.

Here is an examples of this from *Twelfth Night*.

- **You don't see the shipwreck** that brought Viola and her brother to the coast of Illyria at the start of *Twelfth Night*. However, in Act I scene ii **the Captain gives a vivid description** of it and of the perilous position of Sebastian.

- At the same time, the Captain gives Viola some hope for Sebastian's survival. The language of the Captain here has to be realistic about the storm 'our ship did split', but optimistic about Sebastian's chances 'most provident in peril' and 'bind himself... to a strong mast.'

our ship did split

most provident in peril

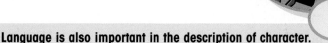

Language is also important in the description of character.

In Act I scene iv of *Twelfth Night*, Viola has become **Caesario**.

- To help the audience recognise Caesario, **Orsino gives a description of how 'he' looks** in lines 29 and 34. Here the emphasis is unwittingly on how feminine 'he' looks, adding to the sense of deception that runs through the play.

Test yourself

Choose one of the following scenes and remind yourself of the event or character being described and its importance to the play.

> **1** Act III scene iii, lines 24-37 of *Twelfth Night*.
>
> **2** Act II scene i, lines 117-127 of *Henry V*.
>
> **3** Act IV scene iii, lines 38-48 of *Macbeth*.

Check the facts

The theatre-going audience of Shakespeare's time were keen to see plays written by what they thought of as educated people. This is why there are so many **references to Ancient Rome and Greece** in Shakespeare's plays. The study of these classical civilisations was an essential part of education in Shakespeare's time, and constant reference to them was **proof of the writer's educated background**.

Puns and word-plays

> **Puns and word-plays are a humorous use of words that sound the same but have different meanings.**

Using puns and word-play was also part of being well-educated. It was considered an art to be 'witty' and make entertaining plays on words to amuse other people.

In Act I scene v of ***Twelfth Night***, **Maria** plays with **the language of sailing** to suggest that Viola moves on.

- Viola proves she is every bit as clever as Maria. In her reply, she continues the pun by insisting on staying 'hull here a little longer' and reminding Maria of her lower position by calling her 'good swabber.'

Earlier, in Act I scene iii between lines 27-33, **Maria plays with the word 'gifts'** when referring to Sir Andrew's lack of them.

> ...he hath the gift of a coward to allay the gust he hath in quarrelling

- The use of language here helps to establish the characters of both Maria and Sir Andrew. The reader is not surprised when Maria is able later to dupe Malvolio; or when Sir Andrew is so easily tricked shortly afterwards.

Test yourself

Find examples of word-play in your chosen play where the character is:

- a) giving a clever reply
- b) insulting or baffling someone.

Shakespeare

Check the facts

> **Shakespeare's plays were not meant to be read in a book but were written to be performed on a stage, usually a bare stage.**

When reading Shakespeare's plays, you need to remind yourself of **how the scenes work as drama**. The best way to do this is to **see various productions of your chosen play**, either in the theatre or on film. Notice how different directors have developed the dramatic effects of scenes.

Act II scene i of **Macbeth** is a good example. **It dramatically hints at the dark deeds to come**.

• Banquo is still as loyal to the king as he was at the start of the play when he says 'still keep my bosom franchised and my allegiance clear'.

• Macbeth, on the other hand, lies to Banquo by telling him he never thinks of the witches.

• There is a dramatic contrast between the two men who were so similar at the start of the play. The juxtaposition of the loyal and honest Banquo next to the lying Macbeth dramatically stresses to the audience just how far Macbeth has sunk.

You can see the contrast in the characters' words when you read the play, but try to think how a director might **point up the contrast** in the way the characters say their lines as well as their appearance, actions and positions on-stage. You can read more about 'being the director' in Units 75–77.

Test yourself

Select any scene from your chosen play.

Write down the features that you could use to stress its drama to the audience.

You could look at such things as:
• the position of the actors on the stage
• where they put their emphasis on words
• their gestures to each other
• how they actually say their words.

Check the facts

Dramatic irony adds suspense to a play.

> **Dramatic irony is when the author allows the audience to know more about what is happening, or is going to happen, than the characters in the play do themselves.**

It is very effective in creating an air of deception in the play and in adding to the dramatic effect when the character discovers what the audience already knows.

At the beginning of Act I scene vi of **Macbeth**, Duncan arrives at Macbeth's castle.

- The audience know about the **witches' prophecies** and about the plans to murder Duncan that night. Yet Duncan says that the castle 'hath a pleasant seat... and sweetly recommends itself'; that Lady Macbeth is an 'honoured hostess'; and of Macbeth he says, 'we love him highly.'

- The audience recognises **the dramatic irony in Duncan's perception of the castle and its occupants** – which are the direct opposite of the actual situation.

The dramatic effect here is one more example of the **theme of deception** that runs throughout Act I of the play.

Test yourself

Choose one of the following scenes and decide how the dramatic irony works in the scene.

> **1** Act II scene ii, lines 44-51 of Henry V.
>
> **2** Act V scene i, lines 170-186 of Twelfth Night.
>
> **3** Act III scene ii, lines 29-38 of Macbeth.

Check the facts

If you're describing a person or an experience to a friend who has no knowledge of either, you often get over the difficulty by **comparing** them to someone or something similar.

> **When you say someone or something is as or like another, you're using a simile.**

- Shakespeare, like many other writers, uses similes to give you an image or a picture of someone you haven't met, or an experience or feeling you haven't encountered.

- In your exam, it's not enough just to identify similes in the writing; this is comparatively easy.

- To impress the examiner you must **say why the simile is effective** and why you think the writer has chosen those particular words to give you the image.

In Act I scene ii of **Macbeth**, a soldier reports the battlefield feats of Macbeth and Banquo. He describes the time when they were suddenly faced with fresh forces. When asked if this troubled Macbeth and Banquo he replies,

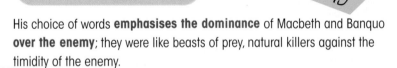

> as sparrows eagles, or
> the hare the lion.

His choice of words **emphasises the dominance** of Macbeth and Banquo **over the enemy**; they were like beasts of prey, natural killers against the timidity of the enemy.

Test yourself

Choose one of the following similes and decide exactly why these particular words have been chosen.

1 Act I scene iii, line 97 of *Twelfth Night*.

2 Act I scene vii, lines 18-19 of *Macbeth*.

3 Act I scene i, lines 27-30 of *Henry V*.

Check the facts

A metaphor is a stronger and **more imaginative comparison** than a simile.

> **While a simile says that something is like or as something else, the metaphor claims that it is actually something else.**

- Metaphors can be more difficult to identify than similes, but you'll still need to show the examiner that you have understood their effectiveness – **why the writer has chosen those particular words.**

Some metaphors are more obvious than others. *Twelfth Night* begins with a famous example:

If music be the food of love

In that line, the character **Orsino links food to love** in a metaphor. He goes on to say that he hopes he will have too much and die of 'overeating'.

- Later in Act V scene i, Orsino uses a more complicated and more hidden metaphor when he says of his approaches to Olivia:

o whose ingrate and inauspicious altars My soul the faithfull'st offerings have breathed out

- This metaphor conveys the image of someone making **an offering at an altar** and finding it rejected.

Both images discussed here express the depth of love **Orsino** feels for Olivia.

Test yourself

Choose one of the following and decide why the metaphor is effective.

> **1** Act III scene i, lines 136-137 of *Twelfth Night*.
>
> **2** Act III scene ii, lines 13-15 of *Macbeth*.
>
> **3** Act IV, the Prologue, lines 2-4 of *Henry V*.

Shakespeare

BBC KS3 Check and Test: English

Shakespeare

Check the facts

- Shakespeare often uses imagery to express the feelings of a character or to describe something.

- Sometimes these are single images, but often **Shakespeare links images together so that patterns emerge.**

- On these occasions you can talk about the imagery of a passage or a speech or even a whole play.

Look at the garden scene in *Twelfth Night* in Act II scene v.

- As the pompous steward, Malvolio, begins to be caught out by Maria's trickery, you can see a **pattern of images** emerging between lines 115 and 128.

- The **references** are to **hunting** and of **hounds** sniffing out their prey. The imagery is of the 'hound' Malvolio sniffing out his 'prey', the assumed love of the Lady Olivia.

> *...he is now at a cold scent.*

> *Sowter will cry upon't for all time, though it be as rank as a fox.*

The extended pattern of images creates a far stronger impact than a single, simple image.

Test yourself

Find for yourself imagery of one of these:

a) love in *Twelfth Night*

b) nature in *Henry V*

c) disease in *Macbeth*.

What does the pattern of imagery tell you about the feelings of the character in your chosen example?

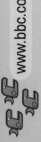

Check the facts

When you think, the images in your mind don't always seem to follow an obvious, rational pattern. For instance, think of the pictures that flash through your mind as you drift off to sleep. They may seem completely random, but if you think about it carefully, you can identify how one thought leads to the next. There is an **internal imaginative logic** to them.

> **You can look for links and meaning even in the wildest imagery to see if there is a logic that gives you clues to the character's state of mind.**

Look at Macbeth's speech in Act V scene v, lines 17-27 of *Macbeth*.

- Macbeth has just been told about his wife's suicide, and his enemies are almost at his castle.

- The images seem wild, as you might expect from Macbeth at this point.

- But examine the things he says more closely and you can link together light, a candle and shadow and begin to understand how his thoughts leap to a shadow player in a theatre and the story he tells.

> *Out, out brief candle!*
> *Life's but a walking shadow...*

There is, in fact, an **imaginative link** that emphasises Macbeth's **mental state** and his **perception** at this point in the play that life is useless and futile.

Shakespeare

Test yourself

Look again at the pattern of images you selected in the previous unit.

Decide if you can see an imaginative link between them.

Does this express the mental state of the character at this point in the play?

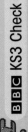

Check the facts

Although you will be mainly answering question on key scenes, you need to **make the examiner aware that you know the whole play.** You can **do this by linking aspects of the key scenes to other major events** in the play.

Look at Act IV scene i of **Macbeth**. Here, Macbeth has returned to the witches to find out what the future holds for him.

Think of the links you can make:

- Macbeth's first meeting with the witches and how it set the tragedy in motion.
- The fact that Macbeth is again given three prophecies and how these develop in the final scenes.
- The prophecy that was made to Banquo and how it still disturbs Macbeth.
- The way the language of the witches again adds to the theme of evil in the play.

It's important to remember to take the opportunity to show the examiner that you know more about the play than just one key scene.

Test yourself

Look again at Act II scenes i and ii of *Macbeth*.

Find at least four points where you can link words or actions to other parts of the play.

Write out the link clearly as it would be used in an exam answer.

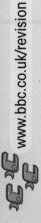

Check the facts

Although you will be mainly answering question on key scenes, you need to **make the examiner aware that you know the whole play.** You can **do this by linking aspects of the key scenes to other major events** in the play.

Look at Act I scene v of **Twelfth Night**. In this scene:

- Olivia finally allows Viola in to listen to Orsino's messages of love.
- Viola has been detained at the gate of Olivia's house by a drunken Sir Toby and by Malvolio.

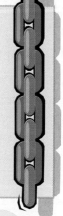

Think of the links you can make:

- Sir Toby's drunkenness causes problems in other parts of the play.
- Malvolio's dismissive attitude to Feste is 'rewarded' later.
- Viola persuades Olivia to disregard the vows she has made after the death of her brother.
- Viola's messages are given in the language of passionate love, a constant theme in the play.

It's important to remember to take the opportunity to show the examiner that you know more about the play than just one key scene.

Test yourself

Look again at Act III scene iv up to line 167 of *Twelfth Night*.

Find at least four points where you can link words or actions to other parts of the play.

Write out the link clearly as it would be used in an exam answer.

Shakespeare

Check the facts

Although you will be mainly answering question on key scenes, you need to **make the examiner aware that you know the whole play.** You can **do this by linking aspects of the key scenes to other major events** in the play.

Look at Act I scene ii of **Henry V**. Here Henry is seeking advice on going to war with France.

Think of the links you can make:

- His debates with the bishops and earls give an early picture of the thoughtful King you see later in the play.

- The gift of the tennis balls is picked up in Henry's later dealings with the Dauphin.

- Henry's decision to go to war links with the characters and preparations that follow.

- The language of the scene emphasises Henry's determined yet thoughtful character, which will dominate the play.

It's important to remember to take the opportunity to show the examiner that you know more about the play than just one key scene.

Test yourself

Look again at Act II scene ii of *Henry V*.

Find at least four points where you can link words or actions to other parts of the play.

Write out the link clearly as it would be used in an exam answer.

Writing

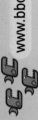

www.bbc.co.uk/revision

Check the facts

- You may get an opportunity in the exam to **assume the role of a character** and to write as if you were that character.

- This question asks you to bring together your thoughts on the character and key events in the play.

- Part of the mark reward will recognise how far your writing develops **a suitable 'voice'** for the character.

Look at **the role of Lady Macbeth** in Act II scene ii of *Macbeth*. You already know about her part in the plot to kill Duncan from Act I.

What aspects of her 'voice' can you see here?

- You could pick up her exhilaration at the start of the scene, followed by worries that the murder has not been done and that their plans will be discovered.

- Then there are her attempts to calm her beloved Macbeth, followed by her cold, calculated planning at the end of the scene.

Writing out these changing feelings as if you were Lady Macbeth, reflecting her desperation for success in your writing, will impress the examiner that you have a clear view of Lady Macbeth's emotional state at this point in the play.

Test yourself

Look again at Act IV scene iii.

> Write down the main points Malcolm might put in a letter to his brother Donalbain explaining:
> - his feelings about events in Scotland
> - his future plans.

Writing

BBC KS3 Check and Test: English

Shakespeare

Check the facts

- You may get an opportunity in the exam to **assume the role of a character** and to write as if you were that character.

- This question asks you to bring together your thoughts on the character and key events in the play.

- Part of the mark reward will recognise how far your writing develops **a suitable 'voice'** for the character.

Look again at Act I scene iv of *Twelfth Night.* Orsino is asking Viola, who is dressed as a young man, to carry his messages of love to Olivia and to ensure she delivers them.

What could you say about his feelings as Viola goes on her way?

- You know that he has already favoured Viola among his courtiers.

- You could pick up on his absolute devotion to Olivia.

- Then, there is his insistence and hope that Viola is allowed to speak to Olivia.

- There is his desire to be alone.

- There's also his promise to Viola of riches if she succeeds.

Writing out these feelings as if you were Orsino, reflecting his burning passion in your writing, will impress the examiner that you have a clear view of **Orsino's emotional state** at this point in the play.

Test yourself

Look again at Act II scene ii of *Twelfth Night.*

Write down the main feelings Viola might put in a diary entry of her visit to the Lady Olivia.

Shakespeare

Check the facts

- You may get an opportunity in the exam to **assume the role of a character** and to write as if you were that character.

- This question asks you to bring together your thoughts on the character and key events in the play.

- Part of the mark reward will recognise how far your writing develops **a suitable 'voice'** for the character.

Look again at Act I scenes i and ii of *Henry V.* Here the bishops are hoping that Henry will decide to go to war with France.

What could you say about the feelings of the Archbishop of Canterbury at the end of the scene?

- You could point to his worries at the loss of valuable church lands and his reflections on Henry's changed character.

- You could pick up on his careful approach to the Salic law and the reasons for his offer of cash support.

Writing out these feelings as if you were the Archbishop, reflecting his clear, political voice in your writing, will impress the examiner that you have a clear view of Canterbury's ideas on war with France.

Test yourself

Look again at Act II scene ii of *Henry V.*

Write down the main feelings one of the conspirators might put in a final letter while he's awaiting execution.

BBC KS3 Check and Test: English

Shakespeare

Check the facts

- You may get an opportunity in the exam to **take the role of a director** and write about the way in which you would direct the production of a key scene.

- For this question, not only do you need to show **an awareness of events, characters and feelings**, but also you need to think about such issues as **the speaking of lines, positions on stage, gestures and props**.

Look again at Act II scene i of *Macbeth*.

How would the director approach this scene?

- You could point to the emphasis on darkness at the start of the scene and think about how the lighting could accent this.

- How would you get over the way Macbeth has sunk as a person compared to the loyal Banquo? You could think about their positions on the stage and exactly how Macbeth tells his lie about the witches.

- Then, in Macbeth's soliloquy, you would need to consider whether or not you want the dagger to be real and visible to the audience, as well as how the references to violence and cruelty could be highlighted.

> **You would need to consider all aspects of directing a scene to impress the examiner that you're aware of the dramatic possibilities and how they link to the themes of the play.**

Test yourself

Look again at Act V scene v of *Macbeth*.

Write down the key points that would be in a director's notebook for staging this scene.

Check the facts

Director

Director's notes
- very low lighting
- Banquo on a raised stage

- You may get an opportunity in the exam to **take the role of a director** and write about the way in which you would direct the production of a key scene.

- For this question, not only do you need to show **an awareness of events, characters and feelings**, but also you need to think about such issues as **the speaking of lines, positions on stage, gestures and props**.

Look again at Act I scene iii of *Twelfth Night*.

How would a director approach this scene?

- You could point to the probable drunken condition of Sir Toby when he comes in, his appearance and to some of the sexual aspects of the word-play between him and Maria. How would you handle this for different audiences?

- Then there is the entrance of Sir Andrew and his appearance, his behaviour with the clever and witty Maria and the contrast between them. How would their gestures and movements, their expressions and the way they said their lines emphasise these things?

- Finally, there is the comic dancing. How would you set out the stage to get maximum comic effect from the end of the scene?

> **You would need to consider all aspects of directing a scene to impress the examiner that you're aware of the dramatic possibilities and how they link to the themes of the play.**

 Test yourself

Look again at Act III scene iv, lines 220-317 of *Twelfth Night*.

Write down the key points that would be in a director's notebook for staging this scene.

Shakespeare

BBC KS3 Check and Test: English

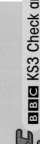

Check the facts

- You may get an opportunity in the exam to **take the role of a director** and write about the way in which you would direct the production of a key scene.

- For this question, not only do you need to show **an awareness of events, characters and feelings,** but also you need to think about such issues as **the speaking of lines, positions on stage, gestures and props.**

Look again at Act IV scene i, lines 35-280 of *Henry V*.

How would a director approach this scene? How would Henry put on his disguise?

- You could point to the entry of Pistol and his attitude to Henry, and Henry's attitude to Llewellyn. How could these be emphasised by the actors?

- You could also think about how the characters could position themselves for the discussion between Henry, Williams and Bates.

- Think about the use of lighting here: how far will their voices and tempers rise, and how will you ensure that the audience sees the swapping of gloves?

- You will need to think about Henry's envy of ordinary lives in his soliloquy. Would you adapt this speech for different audiences?

> **You would need to consider all aspects of directing a scene to impress the examiner that you're aware of the dramatic possibilities and how they link to the themes of the play.**

 Test yourself

Look again at Act V scene i of *Henry V*.

Write down the key points that would be in a director's notebook for staging this scene.

Shakespeare

www.bbc.co.uk/revision

Check the facts

Most lines in Shakespeare have ten or eleven syllables with five heavy stresses and five or six light ones. These lines are called **iambic pentameters** and they reflect the natural emphasis of normal English speech very well.

- Look at the quotation below. The capital letters show the stressed syllables.

> - **If MUsic BE the FOOD of LOVE play ON.**
> - **That FOUGHT with US upON Saint CRISPin's DAY.**
> - **So FAIR and FOUL a DAY i HAVE not SEEN.**

- Look out for irregularities in this stress pattern. They are often used to suggest that the character has confused or disturbed feelings.

Blank verse and rhyming couplets

- Generally, Shakespeare's verse does not rhyme and is known as **blank verse**.

- However, sometimes a verse ends with a **rhyming couplet**. This is where the last two lines of blank verse rhyme. Rhyming couplets alert the audience to a change of scene.

Although Shakespeare generally reserves verse for people of higher rank or for the expression of great passion, this is not always the case. In Act I scene v of *Twelfth Night*, Viola and Olivia speak lines 170-240 in prose and then return to verse.

Test yourself

Select a favourite speech from your chosen play. Try to read it aloud so that the rhythm of the verse reflects the character's mood at that point in the play.

Shakespeare

Shakespeare

Check the facts

> Shakespeare usually uses prose for characters of lower rank or when higher-born characters are talking to those of lower rank.

For example:

- when Macbeth speaks to the murderers in *Macbeth*
- when Henry speaks to Williams and Bates in *Henry V*
- when Olivia speaks to Feste and Malvolio in *Twelfth Night.*

> Shakespeare's other regular use of prose is for comedy.

For example:

- The porter's speech in *Macbeth* Act II scene iii provides an opportunity for comic relief from the drama of the murder of Duncan and its discovery.
- The garden scene in *Twelfth Night* Act II scene v lightens the mood of earnest and passionate love.
- The scenes involving Pistol, Bardolph, Nym and Llewellyn in *Henry V* break up the intensity of war.

- Notice how these scenes are not randomly placed. They often provide **opportunities for momentary relief** for the audience among more serious events.
- Their **position** in the play **emphasises its drama and staging**. They are a reminder to you that the text you're reading is meant to be performed on a stage for an audience.

www.bbc.co.uk/revision

 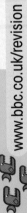

Test yourself

Identify a prose passage in your selected play. Write down why you think Shakespeare has put that passage in prose and what effect you think it has on the drama of the play.

Check the facts

One of the aspects of writing you may be asked to comment on in your exam is **the presentation of a character** in a piece of writing.

> Remember how you think about people's characters in real life:

- how they behave
- what is said about them by people you can rely on
- what they say and how they say it.

> **You can apply these same methods to establish your ideas about characters in fiction.**

Look at this extract from *Angela and Diabola* by Lynne Reid Banks:

> Diabola was now standing on a chair, which she had set on a table, and was busy decorating the ceiling of the room with black-cloaked vampires, fiends and other hideous creatures, half human and half monster, flying overhead. The vicar noticed dazedly that she was using both hands at once. He had read somewhere that this was a sign of evil power.

The writer is trying to establish the character as 'devilish.'

- Even her name sounds like 'diabolic.' The word originally means 'of the devil.'
- Notice what she actually draws.
- Notice also what the vicar – who should know about these things – thinks about her ability to write with both hands.

All of these points help to establish the wicked side of Diabola.

Test yourself

Use the three categories from the top box above as headings for three columns. Now take a central character from a book you have recently read. Try to complete the columns and then summarise your findings on the character.

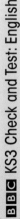

Check the facts

Often in your response to fiction you'll be dealing with **two or more characters** and you'll be asked to **comment on their relationship**.

- Is the relationship friendly?
- Or is it hostile?
- Are the characters afraid of each other?
- Or in fear of what is going on around them?

> **You'll need to be clear about how the writer is presenting the relationship to affect the reader.**

Look at this extract from *Harry Potter and The Goblet Of Fire* by J. K. Rowling. Harry is having breakfast with the Dursleys.

> Dudley looked furious and sulky, and somehow seemed to be taking up even more space than usual. This was saying something, as he always took up an entire side of the square table by himself. When Aunt Petunia put a quarter of unsweetened grapefruit onto Dudley's plate with a tremulous, 'There you are, Diddy darling,' Dudley glowered at her. His life had taken a most unpleasant turn since he had come home for the summer with his end-of-year report.

When you read this extract you can sense some distance between Dudley and Aunt Petunia.

- Look at how Aunt Petunia speaks and Dudley's reaction.
- Look at the adjectives used to create mood – *furious, sulky, tremulous*. The author is trying to present a relationship that is a little strained. Why is the relationship strained at this point?
- Look at the hints about Dudley's size, what he's given for breakfast and the verb used for his reaction.

The author has created a tense mood at what should be a relaxed family meal.

Test yourself

Find an extract from your current class or private book where the writer is using a particular incident to tell the reader about the relationship between characters. Note down your own reactions and think about how the writer is trying to affect the reader's ideas on this relationship.

Check the facts

> Writers use settings in stories to have a particular impact on the reader.

Authors may want to emphasise **danger** or use an **exotic** or **romantic** setting because of the characters or relationships they are writing about.

Look at this extract from *Carrie's War* by Nina Bawden. The children have been frightened while approaching a house through a dark wood, and they finally make it inside the house.

> A warm, safe, lighted place... Hepzibah's kitchen was always like that, and not only that evening. Coming into it was like coming home on a bitter cold day to a bright, leaping fire. It was like the smell of bacon when you were hungry; loving arms when you were lonely; safety when you were scared...

- Notice the adjectives used to compare the kitchen to the wood from which the children have just arrived.

- The writer also uses **comparisons to experiences and feelings you can all recognise**; being hungry and cold and frightened.

- She also uses the **senses of smell and touch** in the comparisons.

All of these devices create a setting to which the reader can relate; but, more importantly, they let the reader recognise and share in the relief and comfort felt by the children. That is the effect the writer is trying to achieve.

Test yourself

Look at books you have read this school year. Find passages that use settings to reflect danger and unhappiness. List the methods – the language and images – the writer uses to affect the reader.

Reading: fiction, poetry and non-fiction

BBC KS3 Check and Test: English

Check the facts

With many extracts, it's not too difficult to see **the writer's intentions when it comes to characters, relationships and settings**. However, there are occasions where the writer wants the reader to do a little more work to establish the writer's intentions. You have to think a bit more carefully to interpret his or her intentions and inferences.

How would you react if you were in charge of appointing a teacher and someone presented the following reference?

Thomas has worked at this school for five years. He is usually on time for his lessons. There have been only a few incidents of major uproar in his class. Some children have done reasonably well in exams. In the afternoons he is often sober.

Would you be impressed? What can you **interpret** from the writing? Perhaps that the candidate:

- is unreliable
- is unable to control a classroom
- is unable to motivate pupils for exams
- has a drink problem?

These facts are not clearly stated but **the writer is surely guiding your ideas with his or her style and type of comments**.

What can you **infer**? **Look at what is missed out**.

- one example is that there is no mention of any contribution to extra-curricular activities such as visits, music, drama or sports teams. The writer wants you to understand that the candidate makes little contribution to school life.

Test yourself

Look in your school or local library for a copy of *Hard Times* by Charles Dickens. Try to interpret what the writer is saying about the school and teacher in the first two paragraphs of Chapter 1.

Can you work out from the writing what it would be like to attend this school?

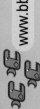

Check the facts

In the exam, you'll almost certainly be asked to comment on **the writer's use of language**. How do you do that?

Look at this extract from *David Copperfield* by Charles Dickens. He is describing the arrival of Miss Murdstone. Dickens certainly wanted the reader to see her as an unpleasant character.

> She brought with her two uncompromising hard, black boxes, with her initials on the lid in hard, brass nails. When she paid the coachman she took her money out of a hard, steel purse, and she kept the money in a very jail of a bag which hung upon her arm by a heavy chain, and shut up like a bite.

How could you comment on the language Dickens used to achieve his effects?

- You could mention the repeated use of the word 'hard'.

- There is also the reference to two hard metals, steel and brass. These words build up a picture of a hard, cold person.

- Her bag is like a 'jail' and there is a rather violent simile at the end.

The reader learns through Dickens's use of language that Miss Murdstone is a harsh, unfeeling and uncharitable woman.

Test yourself

Look in your school or local library for a copy of *Great Expectations* by Charles Dickens. Read the description of Mrs Joe Gargery at the start of Chapter 2.

What comments could you make on the language Dickens uses to affect the reader's view of this character?

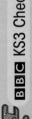

Check the facts

You might be given a poem to read and respond to in your exam.

> **You should approach a poem in the same way as you would approach any other fiction text.**

Although the content might seem mystifying at first glance, most poems are not difficult to understand. However, **you do need to take more care as to how you read them** in the time available before the exam.

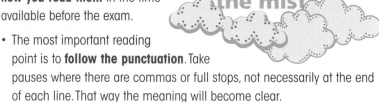

Clearing the mist

- The most important reading point is to **follow the punctuation**. Take pauses where there are commas or full stops, not necessarily at the end of each line. That way the meaning will become clear.

- Reading 'in your head' in this style will also help you to pick up the rhythm of the verse.

Of course, you also need to **work out the content of the poem**. What exactly is the poet writing about?

Test yourself

Pick out three or four poems from a school anthology. Read them 'in your head' following the punctuation.

Now write down one sentence for each, summarising what the poem is about.

Try to be precise about what the poet is writing about.

Check the facts

Most poetry is shorter than prose. Consequently, poets have to be more precise in their use of language. They need to make the words do a lot more work if they are to get across their ideas using fewer words.

> **You need to be aware of the language poets use and its effects.**

Look at the opening lines of Gillian Clarke's poem:
'Miracle on St. David's Day'.

An afternoon yellow and open-mouthed
with daffodils. The sun treads the path
among cedars and enormous oaks.

First read the lines, following the punctuation.

The poet is setting the scene of a fine early spring day. How does she use the language to create this effect?

- Daffodils are an early spring flower and she talks about their colour and shape to express freshness, wonder and delight. 'Yellow and open-mouthed' seems to suggest both the season and our general feelings about it.

- She mentions the trees and pictures the sunlight spreading through them.

In three short lines she has used elements of a spring day and our pleasure in witnessing one to create a vivid picture in the mind of the reader.

Test yourself

What effects are created by the language in this description of a cold morning in **'Hard Frost'** by Andrew Young?

> Frost called to water 'Halt!'
> And crusted the moist snow with sparkling salt...

Check the facts

> **Poets use alliteration when they put words together which begin with the same letter.**

Alliteration is quite easy to spot in a piece of poetry, but simply spotting alliteration is not enough in an exam. As with other language comments, you must try to explain **what effect the poet is trying to achieve**.

- Occasionally, writers will use alliteration to draw attention to certain key words.

- More often they are using the sounds of the letters for effect.

  Notice how Laurence Binyon, in his poem **'The Burning of the Leaves'**, uses the hard sounds of 'b' and 'r' to remind the reader that **leaves in autumn are crisp and crackly**.

  > Brittle and blotched, ragged and rotten sheaves!

- The effect is increased with the use of double hard consonants 'g' and 't' in the 'r' words.

On the other hand, Thomas Hardy is trying to create **the effect of a soft snowfall** in his poem **'Snow in the Suburbs'**.

> And there is no waft of wind with the fleecy fall.

- He uses the softer letters 'w' and 'f' to create this effect.

It is these effects that you would need to recognise in an exam answer.

 Test yourself

Look through any poetry anthology in school and find examples of poets using alliteration of soft and hard letters.

Discuss the effects they are trying to achieve with your teacher.

Check the facts

Poets often try to describe their feelings and experiences by making comparisons through similes.

They do this in the same way that you might do this in conversation with a friend. For instance, when describing how you felt, or something you've seen, you might say 'it was just like...'

When using similes, the writer says one thing is 'like' or 'as' something else.

Similes are fairly easy to identify, but you also need to comment on the effect the poet is trying to achieve.

In his poem **'Pigeons'**, Richard Kell uses some striking similes to remind the reader of how pigeons look.

Strutting like fat gentlemen
With hands clasped
Under their swallowtail coats;
And, as they stump about,
Their heads like tiny hammers
Tap at imaginary nails.

The use of similes creates a clear and humorous picture for the reader of the shape and movement of the pigeons as they look for food in the street.

Test yourself

Think about the effects of similes in Ted Hughes' poem **'The Jaguar'**.

The parrots shriek as if they were on fire, or strut
Like cheap tarts to attract the stroller with the nut.

Check the facts

Metaphors are another form of comparison used by poets.

> **Instead of saying one thing is like or as another thing, metaphors work in a more creative way by asking the reader to imagine that one thing is actually something else.**

What effects do metaphors have on the reader?

Sometimes the metaphor is comparatively easy to identify when the writer clearly says that one thing is another as in Alfred Noyes' poem **'The Highwayman'**.

> The road was a ribbon of moonlight.

- This gives the reader a clear picture of a dark and lonely, moonlit road.

On other occasions you have to think a little harder.

S. J. Tessimond describes a summer day in **'A Hot Day'**.

> A tree, June-lazy, makes
> A tent of dim green light.

- Here the comparison is between an overhanging tree and a tent shading a patch from the hot June sun.

- Only pinpricks of light filter through the branches that would be heavy with leaves in June in this imaginative use of metaphor.

Test yourself

What is the effect of the **metaphors** in these lines from Robert Frost's poem **'The Runaway'**?

You could also comment on the use of a **simile** and the **alliteration**! He is describing a wild horse running away in the snow.

> We heard the miniature thunder where he fled,
> And we saw him, or thought we saw him, dim and grey
> Like a shadow against the curtain of falling flakes.

Check the facts

Sometimes poets link several images, similes or metaphors together. Often a pattern will emerge where the comparisons seem to follow a theme or train of thought.

> When you spot sustained imagery in a poem, you can comment on it. Write about how all the comparisons appear to be on a similar topic and what effect this has.

Look at these lines from Seamus Heaney's poem **'Follower'**, where he's writing about his father's skill at ploughing, not with a modern tractor but with a team of horses.

> His eye
> Narrowed and angled at the ground,
> Mapping the furrow exactly.

- Here the images are all to do with measuring accurately as if you were drawing a map.

- The effect is to emphasise the great skill of his father; the way he ploughs precise furrows while controlling a team of powerful horses.

Seamus Heaney's imagery gives a clear picture of his father as **a strong and expert ploughman**.

Test yourself

What is the effect of the imagery of Miss Creedle in these lines from Gareth Owen's poem **'Miss Creedle Teaches Creative Writing'**?

> Miss Creedle whirls about the class
> Like a benign typhoon
> Spinning from one quailing homestead to another.

Reading: fiction, poetry and non-fiction

BBC KS3 Check and Test: English

Check the facts

> It's important when commenting on fiction, whether prose or poetry, to support your ideas with quotations from the text.

In an exam, the marker needs to see where your ideas have come from. **Quotations do not need to be lengthy, but they do need to be appropriate and relevant to the point you're making.**

You can set out your quotations in one of two ways:

- You can make your point and then add the appropriate quotation, like this:

> We know that Harry Potter has been disturbed by his vivid dream. At the start of Chapter 2, the writer tells us that 'Harry lay flat on his back, breathing hard as though he had been running.'

- You can also put your quotation into the sentence where you're making your point, like this:

> Harry is also aware that something is wrong because 'the lightning-bolt scar' was hurting him 'under his untidy black hair.'

It doesn't matter which style you use as long as the examiner can clearly see where your information on the story or poem has come from.

Test yourself

Practise both of the above methods.

Make comments on a character in a book you have recently read and support your ideas with appropriate quotations.

Check the facts

> When you're not using direct quotations, you still need to support what you've learnt about a text by making references to it.

- Sometimes this might mean **referring to specific events** in a story or lines in a poem and discussing those points
- **OR** it might mean **giving an overview** of a book, play or poem.

> A good overview will demonstrate that you understand the sequence of events or feelings in a text.

- To do this, you'll need to learn the skill of summarising. Instead of repeating a whole text line by line, make brief, pertinent references to key points in the text.

Summarising saves time. Always remember to be aware of the time during your exam.

The cover sheet of the exam paper will give you guidance for each question. Use it and try to stick closely to the recommended times for each of your answers.

Test yourself

Look again at the first chapter of any book you have read in school this year.

Write a brief overview of what has happened with references to the key events.

Reading: fiction, poetry and non-fiction

BBC KS3 Check and Test: English

Check the facts

Non-fiction comes in a variety of formats. It might be a piece of lengthy prose or a short and punchy leaflet. The non-fiction writer might be trying to affect your opinion on some subject or simply wanting to give you information. **Whatever the form or purpose, pictures can play a large part in the effect on the reader.**

Your comments on pictures need to focus on two areas:

Child in need

• Content

Is the picture there to supply you with extra information? Or is it trying to persuade you to a point of view with a content that works on your emotions?

Think of leaflets you have seen for animal protection or child cruelty in regard to this second, more emotional use of pictures.

• Positioning

Where is the picture placed in the text? What impact does it achieve by being placed there?

Think of the way a picture of an attractive model may be placed next to a suggested diet on a health and fitness leaflet.

Animal care

If he was yours

HEALTH
Get On Track For Fitness

Comments on content and positioning will show the examiner that you understand the effect pictures can have on the reader.

Test yourself

Collect a variety of leaflets that come in the post, either appeals or newspaper supplements.

Try to work out the purpose of any pictures used, focusing on content and positioning in the text.

Check the facts

Pictures are just one type of layout feature you might find in a non-fiction text.

Look at the pages of a teenage magazine. Here you will recognise many different features that are used in presenting – or laying out – information or ideas to you.

You might see:

- Headlines and the use of different fonts.
- Boxing – putting lists of facts or ideas in separate boxes next to the appropriate section of text.
- Diagrams – these may be pie charts or bar charts used to get information over visually.
- Cartoon characters and/or speech bubbles.

You'll probably find many more in the magazine.

> In an exam, you need to show that you can recognise layout features and comment on their purpose – to present information and ideas in a range of accessible ways.

Test yourself

Look at a variety of pages from teenage, sports or hobby magazines.

List as many examples as you can of different layout features.

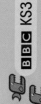

Reading: fiction, poetry and non-fiction

Check the facts

Non-fiction texts are often broken up with **pictures** and **special layout features** to make them more attractive and accessible to the reader.

Try to find a school textbook from twenty or thirty years ago and compare it with a new textbook on the same subject. You'll see a huge difference in the way that the information on the subject is presented.

Nowadays, there is more of an attempt to 'guide' the reader through the text rather than giving them a solid block of information such as you might find in an old textbook.

How is this done?

What you'll need

The questions

- How many prickly pears are you going to buy?
- How many will Pedro have left on his stall?
- How can you work it out?
- Can the 100 square help you to work it out?

Prickly pears are sold two for the price of one so double the number on your card.

Follow up

Make sure that the children have understood the core teaching.

Give out the copy sheets.

Variations:

Include a Dealer Card: Dealer buys half of the lemons that are left.

Resources:

- Jumbo jet sheet, resource sheet 12
- two dice
- labelled
- sheets E,F,J,K,L
- record sheet

- **Subheadings** are usually used to break up the text into smaller, more manageable chunks.

- **Bullet points** might be used to list information in a more direct way.

- **Arrows** might be used to guide you from one section to another.

- **Summary boxes** might be used to condense sections of information.

You need to know the kinds of features that act as signposts, guiding you through the text.

In the exam, you'll be expected to **identify these signposts and comment on their purpose** as tools for the reader.

Test yourself

Ask the oldest teacher in your school to borrow his or her oldest textbook.

Now find the most up-to-date one covering the same topics.

Identify one area of the subject and compare its presentation in the two books.

www.bbc.co.uk/revision

Check the facts

> The style of non-fiction prose is determined by its purpose.

To write about the style, you must first think clearly about the purpose of the text.

What is this writing trying to achieve?

Who is it written for?

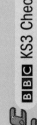

- An **instruction manual** needs to give clear instructions written in a **straightforward style**, so it will be written in short sentences and with a basic vocabulary.

- An **election leaflet** asking you to vote for a particular candidate will use a **persuasive style**. It will employ emotive words which affect your feelings on important issues.

You'll need to identify clearly the purpose of a piece of non-fiction prose in the exam. Then you can **show the examiner that you understand how the style of writing is suitable for the purpose of the text**.

Test yourself

What are the purpose and style of the following non-fiction prose texts?

> 1 A selection of recipes
>
> 2 A sports report
>
> 3 A school prospectus
>
> 4 A leaflet pushed through your letter box asking you to join an animal rights group.

Reading: fiction, poetry and non-fiction

BBC KS3 Check and Test: English

Check the facts

No matter what the purpose of a piece of non-fiction prose, the writing will have a specific structure.

The information or ideas will be presented in **a well-chosen order** so that their meaning is clear to the reader.

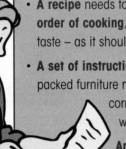

- **A recipe** needs to structure information to match the **order of cooking**, otherwise the food will not look – or taste – as it should.

- **A set of instructions** to assemble a piece of flat-packed furniture needs a structure which follows the correct **order of assembly** or the buyer will be baffled.

  An account of an event may follow the **chronological order of events or**, perhaps, the **different feelings of the crowd** as they watch it.

Whatever structure the writer chooses, it should fit the purpose of the writing.

In an exam, use the purpose of the writing to identify the structure. You can then show the examiner that you **understand the link between structure and purpose**.

Test yourself

Pick out three different types of articles from a newspaper, for example, a sports report, an editorial and a news report.

Identify the structure used in the writing and link it to the purpose of the article.

Check the facts

There are several points about the **use of language** in **informative writing** that you can make.

- The writing should be **clear** with no possibility of misunderstanding.
- The language ought to be **interesting** to keep the reader's attention.
- The amount of technical **vocabulary** – words only associated with the subject of the article – will have to be **matched to the readers' abilities**. Are they experienced in this subject or simply interested beginners?

Look closely at **the sentence style**.

- They are usually **short** to avoid the possibility of misunderstanding.
- **Paragraphs** may contain **only one sentence or one step** in the process.
- **Bullet points** are often used instead of sentences.

All of these points are worth commenting on in an exam to show the examiner that you recognise the language style of a piece of informative writing.

Test yourself

Look at a set of instructions on a microwave meal from the supermarket.

Do they follow the language points made in this Unit?

Reading: fiction, poetry and non-fiction

BBC KS3 Check and Test: English

Check the facts

Writing that tries to persuade you to a point of view will use language aimed at your feelings.

This is called **emotive language**. It plays on your emotions and tries to get you to share an idea or a personal experience with the writer.

- **Ideas**: words will often be replaced with those with similar meanings, but with **stronger effects**, for example:

  ravenous for hungry

  slaughter for kill

  or may make dramatic and moving comparisons:

  the area devastated by the earthquake is like a model village smashed by an angry fist.

- **Shared experience**: words will often represent **extreme emotions**, for example:

  passionate or *loathed*

  or, again, dramatic comparisons :

  swimming with dolphins felt like a time in a natural heaven.

The examiner will expect you to identify these pieces of persuasion and to comment on how they try to affect the feelings of the reader.

Test yourself

Find a piece of persuasive writing. It could be either an appeal to you or an account of a personal experience. Use a highlighter to mark uses of emotive language and replace them with more basic and straightforward words.

Now compare the two versions and identify the different effects on the reader.

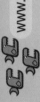

Check the facts

In some ways, presenting an argument is similar to persuasive writing, but it should also attempt to **show both sides of a problem** and **invite the reader to make up his or her own mind**.

The presentation of the problem may include examples of emotive language similar to those you find in persuasive writing.

Examples of this type of writing are:

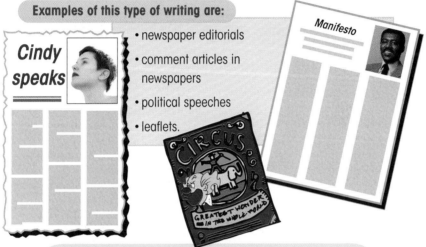

- newspaper editorials
- comment articles in newspapers
- political speeches
- leaflets.

> **You'll need to recognise how the writer presents the argument – one point answering another, or one set of achievements against another.**

- You'll need to be aware of **possible deliberate exaggeration**.
- You'll also need to recognise **the use of link words** in the argument, for example, *however, on the other hand, therefore, alternatively.* These words are called **discursive markers**.

Comments in these areas will show the examiner that you understand how the argument is being presented to influence the reader.

Test yourself

Select an editorial from a daily newspaper.

Use a highlighter to pick out the features of presenting an argument mentioned above.

Answers

02 Spelling

allways (always), writter (writer), storys (stories), friends (friends), fasinated (fascinated), storys (stories), freinds (friends), dident (didn't), bubbleing (bubbling), writter (writer)

1 they're – they are; there – over there, there are; their – belonging to them, their school

we're – we are; where – where is it?, somewhere; were – we were, they were

03 Prefixes

impossible unhelpful disappeared upstairs rethink unsure return supermarket repay exchange unhealthy unsure uptight subtracted extraordinary coincidence discovered postgraduate bicycle

1 insincere dis/reconnect independent im/re/de/ex/compress inedible re/up/downgrade unnecessary dissimilar dis/misspell re/up/mistake prehistoric immature

2 extra – outside, post – behind or after, bi – two or twice, re – repeat or return, ex – out of or former, in – not or without

04 Suffixes

waiting, hopefully, older, laughed, younger, asked, looked, turned, amazement, being, foolish, really, picked, booklet, pointed, gazing, kindest

1 depend (ing, ed, ant), interest (ing, ing+ly, ed, ed+ly, ed+ness), courage (ous, ous+ly, ous+ness), inform (ing, ing+ly, ed, ed+ly, ant, ation), clever (est, ly, ness)

2 Examples: thank (ed, ing, ful, ful+ly, ful+ness, less, less+ly, less+ness), brave (ly, ness, ery), laugh (ed, ing, ing+ly, able, able+ness, ably, ter), thought (ful, ful+ness, ful+ly, less, less+ly, less+ness), attract (ion, ive, ive+ly, ive+ness, er, or, able)

05 Spelling plurals

Words that end in ch, ad es; words that end in a vowel and y, add s; words that end in a consonant and y, change the y to i and add es; words that end in ss, add es; words that end in x add es; words that end in f or fe, change the f or fe to v and add es.

Exceptions: men, feet, children, sheep, oxen, women

1 foxes, babies, thieves, matches, monsters, lives, boxes, losses, mice, cows, places, teeth

2 city, toy, lady, stitch, miss, goal, knife, sheep

06 Punctuation

Have you ever considered how difficult it is to follow writing without punctuation? You don't know where a sentence starts or ends and, on top of that, you can't work out when the writer is asking a question. Punctuation is there for the reader, not the writer. It helps the reader work through a text and understand it.

1 a) exclamation mark b) comma c) full stop d) capital letter e) question mark

2 Have you understood this page so far? If you fail to use punctuation then your words become very difficult to follow, your reader becomes confused and your writing becomes less effective. You must punctuate your writing if you want your reader to understand what you have written. Simple!

07 Apostrophes

1 they have – they've; I had – I'd; do not – don't; should not – shouldn't; can not – can't; she will – she'll; we have – we've

08 Inverted commas

2 (a) One of Macbeth's most famous speeches starts with, 'Is this a dagger that I see before me'.

(b) The witches greet Macbeth as 'king hereafter'.

(c) 'Have you seen the play?' Jackie asked excitedly. Sean turned and replied quietly, 'We're hoping to go and watch it tomorrow'.

09 Sentence forms

1 (a) complex
  (b) compound
  (c) simple
  (d) complex

11 Understanding tenses

1 joke, jokes, am joking, are joking, is joking, joked, was joking, were joking, will joke, will be joking
swim, swims, am swimming, are swimming, is swimming, swam, was swimming, were swimming, will swim, will be swimming
kick, kicks, am kicking, are kicking, is kicking, kicked, was kicking, were kicking, will kick, will be kicking

2 thought, shining, were, pushed, got, looked, saw, knew

12 Which tense when?

Horoscopes claim to tell what lies ahead in the future.

14 Adjectives

white, pinched, startling, jet black, piercing blue, tight sarcastic, thin

16 Adverbs

1 impatiently (How did they stand?); suddenly (When did the crowd surge?); forward (Which way did the crowd surge?); eventually (When did they find their seats?)

2 mysteriously, thoughtfully, happily, generously, rapidly, angrily, easily, wonderfully

18 Creating atmosphere

a trail of smoke puffing cheerily, a thin trail of smoke, a wispy trail of smoke
the warm welcome that lay ahead, the danger that lay ahead, all else was still and silent

25 Linking sentences and paragraphs

first paragraph: Firstly… ; second paragraph: Just below… ; third paragraph: Finally…
sentence links: bus – cliff tops – view – details of view;
cliff top – steps – fear of breaking ankle – being stranded;
arrive at bottom – collapse exhausted

49 Drafting and checking

The first week disappeared quite quickly as there was so much to do. We had to unpack all the cases, hang curtains and make the house as nice as we could. Then we had to start at our new school. Having left so many good friends behind, I wasn't looking forward to this bit at all.

51 Narrative: *Macbeth*

Unnatural events are occurring, for example, a falcon has been killed by an owl and Duncan's horses are eating each other. These bad omens reflect the chaos in Scotland after the killing of Duncan.

52 Narrative: *Twelfth Night*

Antonio's giving of the purse to Sebastian. Antonio's history of fighting against Orsino.

53 Narrative: *Henry V*

They conspired with France to kill Henry in Southampton before he left for France.

54 Character: actions

1 Henry can be cunning and ruthless.
2 Lady Macbeth is practical and calm after the killing.
3 Sir Toby is a clever trickster.

55 Character: what's said about them

1 Sir Toby enjoys a good time.

2 Lady Macduff sees Macduff's flight as madness, fear or lack of love. Ross sees Macduff as someone who knows best what to do.

3 Henry has never harmed his friends, but they question his opinion of Falstaff.

56 Character: what's said by them

1 Macbeth is aware of his own dangerous ambitions.

2 Olivia is prepared to let destiny take its course.

3 Henry feels the heavy responsibility borne by a king.

60 Language: setting

1 Similes on the word 'dark' emphasise the darkness of the setting.

2 Spells and magic point to the ruination of Macbeth.

3 Images create a setting of battle and struggle.

61 Language: description

1 Antonio's struggles with Orsino and his subsequent part in the mistaken identities.

2 John Falstaff and the effect of his death on ideas of Henry's character.

3 Malcolm's plans to invade Scotland and his testing of Macduff's sincerity before he takes him on board.

64 Dramatic irony

1 Chorus has told of their treason so you realise they are condemning themselves.

2 You are aware of the Viola/Caesario/Sebastian confusion.

3 You know of the plot to kill Banquo.

65 Imagery: similes

1 The simile explains how pale blonde is Sir Andrew's hair.

2 Angels emphasise the saintliness of Duncan's character.

3 The kingly nature of Henry is emphasised in contrast to his wild youth.

66 Imagery: metaphors

1 The imagery expresses Caesario's growing to maturity.

2 The snake emphasises the danger and poison of his ambitions.

3 The apprehensions of the night before battle are highlighted.

69 Key scene links: *Macbeth*

Reference to the prophecies of the witches, comparison of the characters of Banquo and Macbeth, reference to the plans for the killing, coldness of Lady Macbeth.

70 Key scene links: *Twelfth Night*

Olivia's sadness, Malvolio's appearance, reference to the letter placed by Maria, Sir Toby's revenge on Malvolio.

71 Key scene links: *Henry V*

reference to treachery, setting out for France, perception of Henry, reference to the responsibilities of the king

72 Writing in role: *Macbeth*

Scotland is suffering under Macbeth and his vices, the testing of Macduff, the plans to invade, his reaction to the slaughter of Macduff's family.

73 Writing in role: *Twelfth Night*

Her puzzlement about her conversation with Malvolio, her realisation of Olivia's feelings, Olivia's manner of speaking, her resolution to let Time sort the matter out.

74 Writing in role: *Henry V*

1. regret for actions – explain the conspiracy. 2. admiration for Henry. 3. surprise at how this youthful king can be so cunning and experienced in the ways of conspirators.

75 Directing a scene: *Macbeth*

The staging of the castle, the impact of crying women, the delivery of Macbeth's speech lines 17-27, the effect of the news about Birnam Wood.

76 Directing a scene: *Twelfth Night*

The confidence of Toby and confusion of Viola, Fabian's contribution, Toby's attitude to Andrew, and the comedy and cruelty of the tricks.

77 Directing a scene: *Henry V*

The appearance of Fluellen, the fight of Fluellen and Pistol, the humiliation of Pistol, the tone of the final words between Gower and Pistol.

83 Interpretation and inference

The language suggests the discipline of the school and the lack of imagination.

84 Reading fiction: language

The language stresses the hardness of her nature, lack of approachability.

86 Reading poetry: language

The language emphasises the frost stilling water into ice and the hardness of the surface.

88 Reading poetry: similes

For example: lets the reader hear the sounds through the words 'shriek' and 'fire'. Lets the reader see the style of walking through the words 'strut' and 'cheap tarts'.

89 Reading poetry: metaphors

The metaphor stresses the sound of hooves, the simile emphasises the intensity of the snowstorm, the soft sounds of the alliterated words reflect softness of snow flakes.

90 Reading poetry: sustained imagery

The effect of the imagery is to show Miss Creedle as a strong natural force assisting the nervous pupils to write more effectively.

96 Reading non-fiction: style

1 information
2 information, but also possibly opinion
3 information, but also possibly persuasion
4 persuasion

Acknowledgements

Every effort has been made to trace the copyright holders of the material in this book. If any omissions have been made, we would be happy to rectify them. Please contact us at the address on the title page.

'The Spring' by Peter Dickinson, from *Touch and Go*, by permission of Macmillan Children's Books.

Natural Disasters: Volcanoes by Philip Steele, 1999. ISBN 1 86007 110 4.

Reproduced by kind permission of the publishers ticktock Publishing Ltd., Century Place, Lamberts Road, Tunbridge Wells, Kent, TN2 3EH

Differences by Richard Kell published by Chatto & Windus. Reprinted by permission of The Random House Group Ltd.

Extract from *Abomination*, © Robert Swindells. Published by Transworld Publishers, a division of the Random House Group Ltd. All rights reserved.

What's inside you? by permission of Usborne Publishing, 83-85 Saffron Hill, London EC1N 8RT, UK. © Usborne Publishing Ltd. 1991.

Harry Potter and the Goblet of Fire. Copyright © J. K. Rowling 2000.

Extract from *The Oxford Children's Thesaurus*, by permission of Oxford University Press.

Cooking in Casserole © Hamlyn.

Article 'Big City Eyes' reproduced with permission of Atlantic Syndication.

Carrie's War by Nina Bawden (Puffin 1974), p.46. © Nina Bawden, 1973. Reproduced by permission of Penguin Books Ltd.

Chinese Cinderella by Adeline Yen Mah (Puffin, 1999), p. 124. © Adeline Yen Mah, 1999. Reproduced by permission of Penguin Books Ltd.

Holes by Louis Sachar, 1999. Reproduced by permission of Bloomsbury Publishing.

The Cambridge Encyclopaedia by David Crystal, 1994. Reproduced by permission of Cambridge University Press.